DOWN BEER STREET

MIKA RISSANEN
JUHA TAHVANAINEN

DOWN BEER STREET

HISTORY IN A PINT GLASS

TRANSLATED BY RUTH URBOM

SOUVENIR PRESS

Souvenir Press Ltd gratefully acknowledges the financial assistance of
FILI – Finnish Literature Exchange

F |
L **I**

First published in Great Britain under the title *Down Beer Street*
in 2016 by Souvenir Press Ltd, 43 Great Russell Street, London WC1B 3PD
First published in Finland in 2014 by Atena under the title *Kuohuvaa Historiaa*
English language translation copyright © Ruth Urbom, 2015

ISBN 9780285643376

Typeset in Caslon by M Rules
Printed and bound in Denmark by Nørhaven, Viborg

CONTENTS

CONTENTS

CONTENTS

Wie das pier summer vñ winter auf dem Land sol geschenckt vnd prawen werden

Item Wir ordnen/setzen/vnnd wöllen/ mit Rathe vnnser
Lanndtschafft/das füran allennthalben in dem Fürsten-
thumb Bayrn/auff dem lande/auch in vnsern Stettñ vñ
Märckthen/da deßhalb hieuor kain sonndere ordnung ist/
von Michaelis biß auff Georij/ain maß oder kopffpiers
über ainen pfenning Müncher werung/vñ von sant Jor-
gentag/biß auff Michaelis/die maß über zwen pfenning
derselben werung/vnd der enden der kopff ist/über drey
haller/bey nachgesetzter Pene/nicht gegeben noch außge-
schenckht sol werden. Wo auch ainer nit Mertzñ/sonder
annder pier prawen/oder sonst haben würde/sol Er doch
das/kains wegs höher/dann die maß vmb ainen pfenning
schencken/vnd verkauffen. Wir wöllen auch sonderlichen/
das füran allenthalben in vnsern Stettñ/Märckthen/vñ
auff dem Lannde/zu kainem pier/merer stückh/dañ al-
lain Gersten/Hopffen/vñ wasser/genomen vñ geprauche
sölle werdñ. Welher aber dise vnsere Ordnung wissentlich
überfaren vnnd nit hallten wurde/dem sol von seiner ge-
richtzöbrigkait/dasselbig vas Pier/zu straff vnnachläß-
lich/so offt es geschicht/genommen werden. Jedoch wo
ain Geüwirt von ainem pierprewen in vnnsern Stettñ/
Märckten/oder auf m lande/yezuzeitñ ainen Emer piers/
zwen oder drey/kauffen/vnd wider vnntter den gemayn-
nen Pawrsuolck außschenncken würde/dem selben allain/
aber sonnst nyemandts/sol dye maß/oder der kopffpiers/
vmb ainen haller höher dann oben gesetzt ist/ze geben/ vñ
außzeschenncken erlaube vnnd vnuerpotñ.

Wilhelmus Vrsiuß
Bauarie dux

Gegeben von Wilhelm IV. Herzog in Bayern
am Georgitag zu Ingolstadt Anno 1516

The German Reinheitsgebot, *or 'purity law'*.

TO THE READER

Europeans have long enjoyed their beer – so much so that authorities through the ages have seen fit not only to tax it but also to legislate its production. The German *Reinheitsgebot*, or purity law, enacted in the Bavarian city of Ingolstadt on the 23rd of April 1516 and reaffirmed on many occasions since, stipulates that beer may be brewed from only malted barley, water and hops. This regulation, however, is underpinned by a truly ancient tradition, and the history of beer extends far beyond the boundaries of Europe.

People noticed early on that sprouted grain could become converted to sugars and fermented. The history of beer stretches back as far as humans have engaged in agriculture. Modern research methods have shown that Stone-Age earthenware vessels discovered in the highlands of Iran were used for storing sprouted and fermented grain. While the first instance of malting and fermentation may well have happened by accident when a pot of grain got damp, people soon noticed the good results of fermentation and learned to use them to their advantage. Archaeologists agree that many of the vessels discovered were used expressly for making beer rather than containing malted mash that had happened to start fermenting.

It has even been hypothesised that the skill of making grain into malt and brewing it into beer is what brought yeast into widespread use, so that beer was accompanied on the table by leavened bread. If that is the case, then beer is even older than bread as a basic human foodstuff.

The Sumerians described drinking beer as early as 4000 BCE, and the first recipes explaining how to brew beer from malted grain and pure water date from the third millennium BCE. The cultivators of the fertile fields of Mesopotamia with their elaborate irrigation systems produced and consumed large quantities of beer, which soon became a major commodity. Mesopotamia is where we also find the oldest known regulations concerning the serving and pricing of beer, as well as references to beer playing a role as the inspiration for many significant projects.

Law 108 of the Code of Hammurabi from the 18th century BCE stipulates that beer is to be priced in units of grain, and any tavern-keeper who overcharges for beer – that is, who charges more than the price for the equivalent amount of grain – shall be thrown into the water. Whereas many have waxed lyrical and philosophised about the effects of wine, beer has been the source of great plans. Law 109 of the Code of Hammurabi states that a tavern-keeper who permits conspirators to assemble under her roof without capturing them and delivering them to a court shall be put to death.

In Egypt under the pharaohs, long home to a great many grape vines, beer was considered to be the tipple of drunkards. Many papyrus scrolls preserved to this day contain rebukes of beer-filled revelling in the streets deploring the stench they left behind in the narrow lanes of Egyptian settlements.

As civilisation spread from Egypt to Greece, the Hellenes considered beer to be an entirely barbaric beverage. The Romans shared that view, as grape vines have always produced ample harvests under the benevolent Italian sun. The mere fact that beer was made from barley, which the Romans regarded as animal fodder, rendered it suspect to them. So it's no wonder the Romans considered the Celtic tribes of Gaul and later the Germanic tribes to be utterly uncivilised, as they enjoyed drinking beer made from barley.

In the first century CE the Roman historian Tacitus wrote in his *Germania* of the Germanic people, who drank large quantities of beer while making decisions in matters of war and peace or when deciding on major matters such as sentencing a member of the tribe to death, and then reconvened the following morning to consider the matter again. If they still thought the decision seemed right, it was then implemented. When Tacitus informed his readers by describing beer as barley juice *quodammodo corruptum* – 'spoilt in a particular way' – he was reinforcing the view, widely held in southern European cultural circles, that beer was not a particularly refined tipple.

During the turbulent times following the fall of the Roman Empire, characterised by mass migrations and famines, food and drink culture meant simply having enough to eat. In the early Middle Ages the Catholic Church, having inherited a substantial share of the vanished empire's prestige as well as propagated the machinery of its bureaucracy throughout Europe, carried on many Roman traditions. Thus the view of beer as a vulgar, even barbaric, drink was preserved through the centuries. In a way, the ancient division between the wine- and beer-drinking parts of Europe is still evident today. The core areas of the old Roman Empire are still wine-drinking lands, while those termed beer-drinkers by Julius Caesar and Tacitus – including the British, the Belgians, the Germans and the Nordic countries – continue to drink beer.

Even now beer is sometimes left to bear the label of a bulk product suitable only for intoxication. Those who share that opinion easily forget the diversity of the world of beer, basing their views on cheap, weak lagers which are brought home from the market in the car boot in packs of six, twelve or twenty-four cans.

But beer is also much more than that. This book presents anecdotes from throughout the centuries when beer played a decisive role in the course of history. We also aim to highlight the central role of beer in European culinary cultures and customs, as a source of inspiration and even a facilitator of friendships between nations.

In the twenty-four chapters in this book, we present beer in the context of cultures, ideas, social changes and economic circumstances in different eras. The stories come from all over Europe, ranging from the early Middle Ages to the twenty-first century. At the end of each chapter, we give a more detailed description of a particular beer that is linked to the events described in the chapter. Many of them are available outside their place of origin, so you can experience the frothy history of Europe through your nose and taste buds as well.

And so we'd like to welcome our readers on an enjoyable excursion through the history of beer. Cheers!

21 April 2014
The authors

To stop things getting too dry

In this book we present some background information on the beers mentioned, their connection with the events described in each chapter, their style and characteristics.

ABV: The percentage of alcohol content by volume.

GRAVITY: In mashing germinated grain, or malt, the proportion of the total wort mass that is made up of dissolved sugars. The sugar in the wort is turned into alcohol by the addition of yeast, so in practice a higher gravity will produce a higher alcohol content. This is expressed using the Plato scale (e.g. 10°P means that 10% of the wort mass is sugar.)

BITTERNESS: The bitterness from hops in beer, measured according to the EBU scale (EBU = *European Bitterness Units*). The higher the value, the greater the bitterness.

COLOUR: The hue of the beer, measured according to the EBC scale (EBC = *European Brewing Convention*). The higher the value, the darker the beer.

The table below lists the values for four well-known beers from Finland, our home country.

	Karjala (brewed in Lahti)	Sandels Tumma (brewed in Iisalmi)	Keisari EloWehnä (brewed in Nokia)	Koff Porter (brewed in Kerava)
TYPE	lager	dark lager	wheat beer	imperial stout
ABV	4.5%	4.0%	4.7%	7.2%
GRAVITY	10.3°P	10.6°P	11.2°P	17°P
BITTERNESS	18 EBU	21 EBU	14 EBU	45 EBU
COLOUR	11 EBC	65 EBC	23 EBC	300 EBC

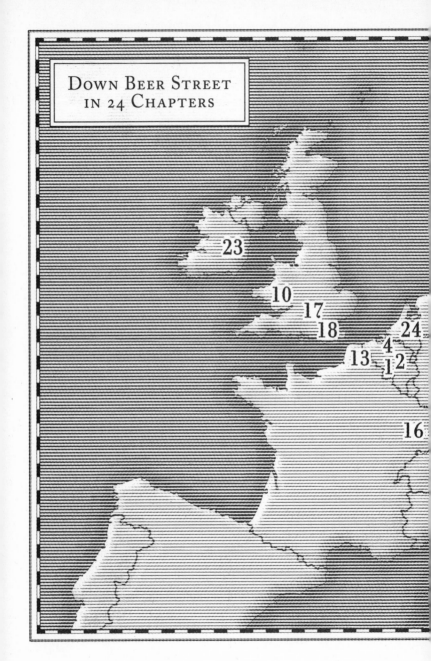

DOWN BEER STREET
IN 24 CHAPTERS

23

10

17

18

24

4

13

1 2

16

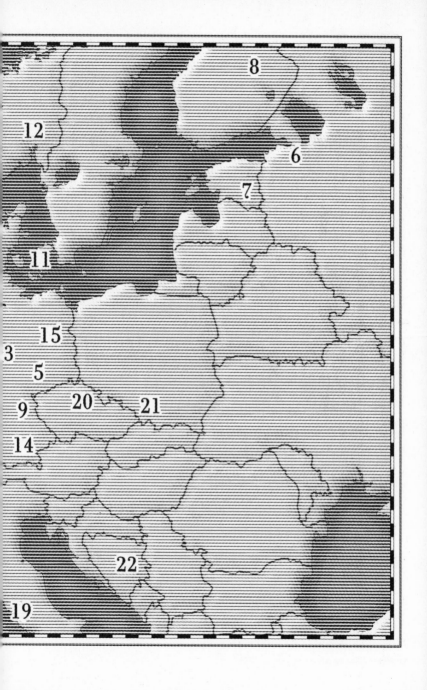

maladies · mais le uler les
estuet si les amendent selo-
res ensegnemens que nous
deisimes en le premiere partie
car por les ensegnemens que
nous deisines fesismes la si n-
en passerons briement.

Illustration from a 13th-century manuscript.
A monk tasting some beer in a cellar.

I

Beer and the Church: A holy alliance

The sacred scriptures of Christianity were collected in a region where little barley was grown, and this is evident in the content of the Bible. Jesus didn't turn water into beer at the wedding at Cana, and there was no tankard passed round at the Last Supper. Early Christians followed the example of the Good Book and drank wine.

Beer had long been shunned in southern Europe even before the arrival of Judaeo-Christian beliefs. The earliest written accounts of beer drinking in Europe date from the 7th century BCE, when the Greek poet Archilochus told of Thracians who drank 'barley wine'. The Greeks' attitude towards other nations was haughty, to say the least, and it extended to their views of those barbarians' customs, including their food and drink. Wine was considered to be a gift from the god Dionysus to the impoverished human race. Meanwhile, there is not a single favourable account of beer – the barbarians' beverage – to be found anywhere in Greek literature.

The Greeks' critical views of the taste and detrimental health effects of malt beverages were handed down to the Romans, who spread them to the areas they conquered between 133 BCE to 117 CE, from the Middle East as far West as Britain. The northern boundary of the Roman Empire did not constitute a stark dividing line between beer- and wine-drinking cultures, though. In territories such as Gaul (present-day France and Belgium), Hispania (now Spain and Portugal) and Britain that were under Roman rule, the Celts kept their beer traditions alive. The upper class preferred to fill their cups with wine. As regions became more Romanised, the less beer was brewed there.

The rise of Christianity as the state religion of the Roman Empire in the 4th century CE hastened this change. Wine had its adherents in both the Judaeo-Christian and the Graeco-Roman traditions. In the 5th century Saint Cyril of Alexandria described beer as 'the Egyptians' cold, cloudy beverage which causes incurable diseases'. Wine, on the other hand, 'gladdens man's heart', as it says in the Psalms. As an aside, we will mention that very same Cyril expelled the Jews from Alexandria, incited the murder of the influential female philosopher Hypatia and destroyed some of Alexandria's libraries, so you can draw your own conclusions about his judgement.

The mass migrations in the 4th and 5th centuries took Germanic tribes across the Danube and Rhine. Those tribes had been accustomed to slaking their thirst with beer since their very beginnings. They converted to Christianity early on and acquired the customs of the areas where they had settled. The Germanic peoples did not stop drinking beer completely, though the ruling class and the Church's scholars deemed wine more worthy. The same division between the rulers and the common people in their choice of drink was also reflected as the Germanic peoples settled throughout central Europe. In places where grapes did not grow, aristocrats sourced wine as a sought-after import from the South. Beer was labelled a second-class drink in continental Europe, until the situation was rescued by the brilliant Irish.

Since the times of Gaius Julius Caesar, the Roman legions had launched occasional invasions and explorations from Gaul over the English Channel into Britain. The southern and central parts of Britain were finally annexed into the Roman Empire in 43 CE. The main reason behind the Romans' eagerness to conquer Britain was their desire for its metal reserves, which turned out to be smaller than they had hoped. The Romans advanced as far as the Scottish Highlands, but they left the neighbouring island of Ireland in peace.

The Celts were able to live in peace on their island at the edge of the known world until the 5th century, when the British-born missionary Patrick (ca. 387–460) came to spread the Christian religion among the Irish. No details have been preserved about St Patrick's own preferences, but his pupils wasted no time in combining Irish beer tradition with the newly arrived Christian teachings. Every spring Saint Donard (d. 507) brewed a barrel of beer, which he would then serve to churchgoers in Rath Muirbuilc (now known as Maghera) on the Tuesday after Easter. Saint Bridget of Kildare (451–525), one of Ireland's national saints, took a favourable view of beer as well. The legends of her miracles emphasise her hospitality. When a thirsty traveller arrived in Kildare but there was nothing to drink, Bridget transformed her bathwater into beer. And the barrel of beer she sent to one parish multiplied along the way so that there were enough barrels for eighteen churches in all. However, the most impressive evidence of her miracles is to be found in her prayer: 'I would like a great lake of beer for the King of Kings. I would like to be watching Heaven's family drinking it through all eternity.'

Christianity quickly took root in Ireland. Just a few generations after St Patrick, Ireland became one of Europe's main sources of Christian missionaries. Representatives of the Church continued to spread the faith to the remote corners of the British Isles as well as to the European continent. Those Irishmen also took with them their down-to-earth views on the compatibility of beer drinking and spirituality.

Saint Columbanus was born in eastern Ireland around 540. He served in several monasteries in his homeland before leaving for the Continent at the age of 49 to do missionary work. Columbanus was shocked by the state of Christianity in Gaul under the Frankish rulers and resolved to restore doctrinal order to the Burgundian court as well as the common people. He founded the Annegray monastery, which served as a model for many European monasteries north of the Alps in the early medieval period. Though there were some monasteries in Columbanus' homeland of Ireland which had forbidden their monks to consume alcohol, he did not support that ban himself. Quite the opposite, in fact. Columbanus preached asceticism in monastery life, but he valued beer. The holy abbot did not tolerate spillages of beer, and the rules of the Annegray monastery even set out specific punishments that would be meted out to any monk who wasted beer. The careless brother's portion of beer would be replaced with water for as long as was thought necessary to compensate for the amount of beer that had been spilled. Evidence of the central status of beer in Columbanus' monastery can also be seen in the numerous malty legends of his miracles.

One evening when the monks were assembled for dinner, a servant went down into the cellar to fetch more beer. He opened the tap on a barrel and was filling his jug when he heard Columbanus calling him. With a full jug of beer in one hand and the bung in the other, the servant hurried upstairs. When a monk seated at the table happened to ask about the bung, the servant rushed off. He had forgotten to replace the bung in the barrel and ran back into the cellar. A miracle awaited him downstairs. Not a single drop of beer had dripped onto the floor: the barrel was still full to the brim. Relieved, the servant gave thanks to the Lord. The delighted monks explained the occurrence by saying that God wanted to spare the abbot's obedient servant from the punishment decreed in the rules of the monastery. The monks' faith in divine Providence was strengthened, and the dinner could continue in an even more joyous spirit.

Columbanus' reputation as a pious man spread, and he founded more monasteries around Burgundy. His second beer-related miracle occurred at the monastery in Fontaine-les-Luxeuil. As Columbanus' hagiographer Jonas of Bobbio later wrote: 'Columbanus went to the

Fontaines monastery and saw sixty monks working in the fields. When they had finished their arduous labour, he said, "My brethren, may the Lord prepare for you a feast." Upon hearing this, the abbot's attendant replied: "Father, believe me. We have only two loaves and very little beer." "Bring them," Columbanus told him. The attendant brought the loaves and beer to Columbanus, who raised his eyes towards heaven and said, "Jesus Christ, Saviour of the world, who fed five thousand with five loaves, multiply these loaves and this drink!" And a miracle occurred. Everyone could eat his fill and drink as much as he wanted. The servant carried back twice as much in bread crusts and double the original amount of drink.'

Not all beer was good news, though. In 611 on his travels in Brigantia (now Bregenz in Austria) Columbanus heard of an enormous tun of beer the local residents were going to sacrifice to the pagan god Wodan. He went to the square where the tun stood and destroyed it with his breath. The tun splintered into bits and the beer spilled over the ground. It is said that most of the city's residents converted to Christianity as a result. From then on, they knew in whose name beer was to be blessed.

If it was Columbanus who made beer respectable, St Gallus (ca. 550–646) – another monk who had accompanied Columbanus from Ireland to Burgundy – also played a role in its history. Gallus also went on the aforementioned journey to Brigantia with Columbanus, but was taken ill and had to stay in what is now northern Switzerland to recuperate. He enjoyed the area so much that he settled there permanently. After Gallus' death a chapel was built in his memory and later expanded into the abbey of St Gallen. The monks there carried on the Irishmen's traditions. As the decades passed, St Gallen attracted more and more monks and continued to grow and prosper. The plans for the abbey complex, completed around 820, became a model for European monasteries in the High Middle Ages.

Naturally, they took a suitably thorough approach to brewing beer as well. The plans show a detailed layout of the granaries, grain-drying areas, mill, cribs for malted and unmalted grain and the location of the brewery itself. The storage areas for the beer were located in the cellars. In fact, there were three breweries – an arrangement which was also spread to other monasteries along with the plans. The main brewhouse made beer for the abbey's own use, while the second made beer for special guests. The third was designed to quench the thirst of pilgrims and beggars. It is not known exactly what differences there were between the beers brewed in these different breweries. According to the plans, the abbey's own brewery was the only one with a dedicated area for filtering the beer. Clearly, these holy men reasoned that the best beer was for themselves. In August 816 the Aachen synod decreed that the daily ration for a monk was a pint of *good* beer.

The link between monasteries and brewing beer turned out to be a long and fruitful one. In the Middle Ages there was no shortage of novices and postulants arriving at monasteries – not least of all because the material conditions within religious communities were better than outside their walls. Some monks specialised in brewing beer, forming their own valued profession. Over the decades they increased their knowledge of the brewing process, thereby improving the quality of the monasteries' beers. The Frankish empire, which by the early 9th century extended from the Atlantic coast deep into Germany, had a particularly large number of monastery breweries, but breweries were established on the St Gallen model in Britain as well. Irish monasteries had their own brewing heritage, so there was no need to import the Continental model there.

The stabilisation of nations in the late Middle Ages created the right conditions for the creation of commercial breweries. The number of monastery breweries gradually decreased, particularly in the 19th and 20th centuries. On the one hand, commercial breweries' industrial beer production was on a larger scale and more lucrative than before. On the other, fewer people joined monasteries and they focused on their core operations, to borrow a term from the business world. Prayer and spiritual life were regarded as more important than brewing beer.

There were two more paths open to monastery breweries besides closing down. Some chose to focus on small-scale craft brewing, making beer just for their own consumption. Some adopted the contemporary business model and shifted their production in a more industrial, commercial direction. Monastic beers evoke strong images that can be utilised in marketing. In some cases this has led to overstepping the mark, such as when breweries have marketed their products under the names of dissolved or non-existent monasteries. But the invisible hand seems to prune the most egregious charlatans out of the market. These days, Belgium is particularly known for its monastery beers, and the use of monastery names is monitored much more closely there than in other countries. The most authentic tradition is represented by the beers from six Trappist orders, brewed by the monks on the monasteries' own premises. A broader group are certified monastery beers brewed by commercial breweries in coop-eration with monasteries. A few dozen brewery-monastery ventures have been authorised to call their products 'abbey beers'.

Blessed beer

Although Gambrinus is not actually a saint officially canonised by the Catholic Church, this mythical 'king of beer' is considered throughout Europe to be the patron saint of the entire culture of beer – including its drinkers and breweries. According to various legends he received knowledge of how to brew beer from the Egyptian goddess Isis, invented the recipe for beer with hops, and won many contests (emboldened by beer). The truth behind these tales is obscure. The mythical figure may owe his name to the Celtic-Latin word *cambarius*, 'brewer', or the Latin term *ganeae birrinus*, 'one who drinks in a tavern'. A more likely possibility is that the name derives from the Latinised name of a Dutch ruler, *Jan Primus*, or John the First. If that is the case, then the real-life figure behind the name would be either John I, Duke of Brabant (1252–1294) or John the Fearless, Duke of Burgundy (1371–1419).

Lest our topic feel too worldly, we can also raise a glass to the dozens of patron saints of the brewers, hop-pickers and umpteen other groups. The best-known ones are listed below.

Saint	Who were they?	Patron saint of	Feast day
Amandus	Bishop of Maastricht (ca. 584–675)	brewers, innkeepers	6 Feb
Arnold	Bishop of Soisson (ca. 1040–1087)	hop-pickers, Belgian brewers	8 Jun & 14 Aug
Arnulf	Bishop of Metz (ca. 582–640)	brewers	18 Jul
Boniface	missionary (d. 754)	German brewers	5 Jun
Bridget of Kildare	Irish abbess (451–525)	brewers	1 Feb
Columbanus	missionary (ca. 540–615)	Belgian brewers	23 Nov
Dorothea	martyr (d. 311)	brewers	6 Feb
Gambrinus	John I (1252–1294) or John the Fearless (1371–1419)	beer, brewers	11 Apr
Hildegard of Bingen	German abbess (1098–1179)	hop-growers	17 Sep
Martin of Tours	Bishop of Tours (ca. 317–397)	innkeepers, social drinking	11 Nov
Urban of Langres	Bishop of Langres (ca. 327–390)	coopers	2 Apr
Wenceslaus	Duke of Bohemia (ca. 907–935)	Czech brewers	28 Nov

St-Feuillien Triple

LE ROEULX, BELGIUM

TYPE: ale
ABV: 8.5%
GRAVITY: 18.5°P
BITTERNESS: 22 EBU
COLOUR: 12 EBC

Saint Foillan ('Feuillien' in French) was one of many Irish monks who arrived on the European continent in the Early Middle Ages to preach the gospel. He was martyred in 655, when bandits attacked him and his companions in the forest near Soignes. Foillan's remains were interred in the town of Le Roeulx, where a monastery was later established under his name: the *Abbaye St-Feuillien*. The story of the abbey ended in the late 18th century in the upheaval of the French Revolution, but the brewery remained in operation. Now a family firm, the brewery's operations have been managed by four generations of the Friart family in the name of the abbey since 1873.

St-Feuillien Triple is a pale amber abbey ale with a compact head. During its second fermentation in the bottle it develops notes of aromatic hops, a full-bodied flavour and fresh fruitiness, which also covers the taste of the alcohol. It won a Highly Commended rating in the Abbey Ale (Pale) category at the 2009 World Beer Awards.

The Manneken-Pis statue has been passing water in Brussels for centuries. Early 18th-century woodcut by Jacques Harrewyn.

II

The secret of the graceful arc

The Manneken-Pis fountain, a sculpture depicting a small boy urinating at the corner of Rue de l'Étuve and Rue du Chêne in Brussels, is one of that city's most familiar landmarks. The first statue was installed on the site back in the 14th century, but the current model – or another similar to it – has been passing water in the centre of Brussels since 1619.

According to one legend, the secret behind the graceful arc sent forth by the little boy is the local lambic beer

At just 61 cm, the Manneken-Pis is small for a public statue. The micturating lad cannot be considered life-sized, as he is already standing on his own and appears to be around two years old. His posture, leaning backwards slightly, is relaxed yet stable. His cheeks and legs, cast in bronze, still have a toddler's characteristic chubbiness. The title of the sculpture means 'pissing little man' in the local Flemish dialect. The bronze fountain by Jérôme Duquesnoy replaced a 300-year-old stone version in the 17th century. The little sculpture has been stolen numerous times throughout its history, and the original piece is now housed in the safe confines of the Brussels City Museum, located on the Grand-Place. The version that tourists snap photos of on the street corner is an exact copy, installed in 1965.

The medieval Low Countries were a patchwork of nations. Most of the region was formally part of the Holy Roman Empire of the German Nation, but in practice the counts and dukes ruled quite independently over their individual vassal realms. One of the largest states in the region was the Duchy of Brabant, which extended from the centre of what is now Belgium to southern Holland in the 12th century. The duchy was governed from Brussels and Louvain in a way that the more northerly centres of commerce found unconscionable. The burghers of Antwerp and Breda cursed the flow of their tax monies to Brussels, and local nobles were only too willing to stoke the flames of rebellion.

Godfrey III was born as the successor to the throne of Brabant during a period of uncertainty in 1141. The city of Grimbergen, which would later become known for its monastery beer, had already been in rebellion for a few years. Upon the unexpected death of his father, Godfrey II, the following year, the little lad inherited the rumbustious duchy and a grandiose string of titles: 'Count of Louvain, Landgrave of Brabant, Margrave of Antwerp and Duke of Lower Lorraine'. The Berthout family which ruled over Grimbergen rose up in open rebellion. Soon, more noble clans from the northern parts of the duchy started rattling their sabres. An auspicious moment had arrived to overthrow the ruler of Brabant.

Young Godfrey was probably blissfully unaware of the situation. When the northern insurgents began their march towards Brussels in 1142, Godfrey's mother, the dowager Duchess Lutgarde, asked their neighbour for help. Thierry of Alsace, the ruler of the neighbouring county of Flanders, sent a party of soldiers to safeguard Brussels. Their commander, Lord Gaasbeek, had a surprising request for the dowager duchess: 'My lady, if you wish to be sure of a victory, let your son come along onto the battlefield. This request has been made by my troops.' Lutgarde could not afford to refuse. She remained in Brussels, but Godfrey, the army's titular commander who had only just learned to walk a few months earlier, set off to crush the rebellion. The boy ruler was looked after on the journey by a wet-nurse called Barbara.

In medieval times, wealthy families usually employed wet-nurses to supply their children's needs for nutrition in their first eighteen months to two years. People believed that noble ladies were not suited for physical work, which is how breastfeeding was viewed. The use of a wet-nurse also came to be regarded as a status symbol. Even though the pay was meagre, only the upper echelons of society could afford to employ one. It was also generally believed that breastfeeding prevented pregnancy. So if a family wanted to add more heirs quickly, someone other than the new mother was brought in to take care of breastfeeding duties. In practice, wet-nurses also ended up providing a substantial amount of childcare as well.

The Brabantian army progressed a dozen or so kilometres northwards, where they encountered insurgents on the battlefield at Ransbeek, not far from the city of Grimbergen. The troops began to assemble, and it was feeding time for Godfrey. Barbara regularly consumed a full ration of tasty lambic beer – the speciality of Brussels – and she produced plenty of milk.

Over the centuries people have firmly believed that drinking beer increases the production of milk, and even in the early 20th century beer was advertised as a healthy drink for nursing mothers. While we cannot recommend the use of alcohol in conjunction with breastfeeding, there is some scientific evidence that beer increases milk production, though researchers do not fully agree on the matter. One study identified beta-glucan, a long-chained carbohydrate found in barley and oats, as the substance responsible for the effect. The alcohol content of beer does not have a significant effect on the amount of beta-glucan, and the same effect can be achieved with alcohol-free beer, home brew or malt extract. In medieval times, people were not as careful in dealing with alcohol. If Godfrey, just over a year old, fancied something other than breast milk to drink, it is said he had his own wineskin from which he could take a sip of weak lambic.

By the time the troops had assembled into their ranks, Godfrey had a full belly. He was placed in a cradle hung from a tree branch, where the little fellow burped his thanks. Suddenly nature called. Godfrey got up, leaned back slightly and let out a long yellow stream towards the enemy troops.

The Brabantian army cheered their commander-in-chief's heroic feat. The young duke had humiliated the rebels in the worst possible way. He'd shown them the noble family jewels and figuratively pissed in their faces. Once Godfrey had taken care of his business and settled down for his nap, the Brabantian army launched a charge against the insurgents. Their commander's fearless gesture had instilled a desire for victory in his men which the Grimbergen troops could not resist. The Battle of Ransbeek was over quickly. The rule of Brabant was maintained, and the insurgents retreated home to gather their strength for future skirmishes.

The victorious army returned to Brussels in triumph, and the legend of the pissing little fellow spread by word of mouth. Songs proclaimed that the victors were 'Brussels guns as well as lambic'. The soldiers brought the oak tree in which Godfrey's cradle had hung with them as part of the spoils from the battlefield. The tree was planted in the centre of the city, where it was said to have stood for a couple of centuries to commemorate the event. When the oak finally rotted away, Godfrey's noble deed was immortalised in the form of a fountain carved from stone.

The rule of Godfrey III, the Grimbergen rebellion and the Battle of Ransbeek are indisputable historical facts. The pissing story, however, is based on oral sources, so we cannot be completely certain that it really happened.

There are also competing legends behind the Manneken-Pis figure. One has it that the little lad had saved the city from burning down in an arson attack by peeing on a fuse lit by conspirators. Other people believe that a wealthy merchant erected the statue in gratitude for the safe return of his little lost son. The boy was found safe and well, doing what came naturally.

Cantillon Gueuze 100% Lambic Bio

BRUSSELS, BELGIUM

TYPE: lambic
ABV: 5.0 %
GRAVITY: 12.7°P
BITTERNESS: 25.8 EBU
COLOUR: 16 EBC

Lambic beers are produced in a limited geographic area in the Senne river valley in Brussels and to the south-west of the city. There are only around ten or so producers of this traditional type of beer. The hops used in lambics are aged for two to three years so they have lost their sharp edge. Hops are not used to add bitter taste to lambics; rather, they are used for their preservative qualities. One characteristic feature of lambics is that they are produced via spontaneous fermentation through 'wild' yeasts and bacteria in the environment, without the addition of yeast to the wort. After brewing, the wort is cooled in shallow vessels in the open air. Traditionally, the windows in the loft of the brewery are left open so the microbes from the river valley can pass through. Later, the wort with its wild yeasts is transferred into wooden barrels, where the beer is left to ferment and mature until the desired results are achieved. This can take anywhere from a few months to three years.

Gueuze is a blend of new and old lambics, which continues to ferment in the bottle as well. Cantillon Gueuze, produced by a family-owned brewery since 1900, is a blend of one-, two- and three-year-old lambic batches. The ingredients for this organic beer are Pilsner malt, unmalted wheat and two-year aged Hallertau hops. The beer is cloudy and amber-coloured. It has a fairly acidic, wheaty, medium-bodied flavour with characteristic notes of citrus and apple.

In 1510, Martin Luther's study in Coburg had everything he needed,
from beer to books.
19th-century woodcut. Source: Landesbibliothek Coburg.

III

The Reformation had some help from hops

The landscape near the small town of Eisleben offers views of archetypal rural Germany. The rugged Harz mountains rise up in the north-west. In the other directions are hilly farmlands punctuated by small woods and villages with church steeples. Wheat and oats ripple in the fields. Here and there, you can spot deep green hops plantations.

The town's main claim to fame is its connection with the theologian Martin Luther. He was born in Eisleben in 1483 and died there in 1546 at the age of 62. Though they lived in the northernmost areas where grape vines were grown, Eisleben residents did not usually have wine goblets on their tables in the 16th century. They drank beer with their meals, from breakfast all the way to supper. Their weekly portion of wine came on Sunday mornings, administered by the priest at the church altar.

Under the circumstances it is natural that Luther also enjoyed drinking beer. In his student years he frequented the taverns of Erfurt, along with many other young people. Later on, Luther recalled the University of Erfurt as being equally a 'brothel and an alehouse'. In 1508 Luther continued his theological studies in Wittenberg, the beer capital of Saxony, which had around 2,000 residents and 172 breweries. (This impressive ratio is explained by the fact that most of them were home breweries.) His studies went well, and in 1512 young Dr Luther was appointed professor of theology at the University of Wittenberg. Luther's liking for beer was firmly nailed into the annals of ecclesiastical history in 1517, when he published his 95 theses in Wittenberg accusing the Catholic Church of selling indulgences and other improprieties. His theses quickly made their way throughout Europe north of the Alps: in Germany, the Netherlands, Britain and the backward Nordic lands – basically, wherever people drank beer.

The head of the Catholic Church at that time was Pope Leo X, from the powerful Medici family of Florence. He lived like a Renaissance prince of his status and heritage, amply nourishing himself, in the ways of the spirit as well as the flesh. When he was elected Pope, Giovanni di Lorenzo de' Medici celebrated by throwing a four-day party for the residents of Florence in March 1513. Wine was decanted into everyone's jugs from gilded barrels. When the new Pope triumphantly arrived in Rome in April 1513, the city's fountains gushed forth wine instead of water as His Holiness passed by. He already possessed ample personal wealth, but the Catholic Church was constantly in need of more funds in the early 16th century. The reconstruction of St Peter's Basilica in Rome was swallowing up all of Christianity's spare change.

One way of getting funds was by selling indulgences. The practice of cancelling out sins by doing good deeds, such as giving money to the Church, had been employed for centuries, but the sale of indulgences to sinners became more visible in the 16th century than before. In Germany, the Dominican friar Johann Tetzel was particularly successful at marketing statements of mercy. It is, however, uncertain whether he was the source of the slogan *Sobald das Geld im Kasten klingt, die Seele in den Himmel springt* ('As soon as the coin in the coffer rings, the soul into heaven springs').

Luther's theses criticising these indulgences got a chilly

reception in Rome. In 1520 Pope Leo X issued a papal bull to Luther, in which he demanded that the academic change his teachings. When Luther refused to respond to the pope's order and instead publicly burned the missive, he was excommunicated in January 1521. Luther appeared to be destined for the same fate as Jan Hus and John Wycliffe, two earlier figures who had also defied papal authority. Hus was burned at the stake in 1415. Wycliffe managed to die of old age in 1384, but his bones were dug up on the orders of the pope in 1428 and thrown onto a bonfire.

Luther's reprieve came in the form of protection by Frederick III, Elector of Saxony, also known as Frederick the Wise – another beer aficionado. Pope Leo X respected Frederick and his political influence and did not unleash any harsher measures against those living under the Elector's protection. Frederick III organised a hearing for Luther to publicly advocate his views at the Diet of Worms in April 1521.

In the town of Worms on the Rhine, visitors were served only wine. Luther's friend, Eric I, Duke of Brunswick-Lüneburg, was aware of this. He wanted to make Luther feel as much at home as possible in the Rhineland while he was preparing his defence, which could literally be a matter of life and death. The duke sent a barrel of Einbeck beer to Worms. Later on, Luther often recalled this gesture with gratitude. The hearing at the Diet of Worms was a success for Luther – in a way. He did not recant his statements, which led to his final excommunication from the Church. He would no longer reform the Catholic Church from within. Against his will, he would have to found a new, Protestant, denomination. In the eyes of his supporters, after the Diet of Worms Luther was entitled to wear the halo of a religious leader as well as the robes of a secular martyr. Holy Roman Emperor Charles V declared Luther a traitor to the Empire, a man who should be arrested upon sight.

Rumours were circulating that assassins had killed Luther, but in fact he was in hiding in Frederick III's Wartburg Castle. When the worst of the uproar was over, Luther returned to Wittenberg in 1522. Under Frederick's protection, Luther could live there relatively freely, as he had done before the publication of his theses – enjoying the occasional beer at home and in taverns. To his critics, Luther stated that it was 'better to sit in the tavern thinking about church than to sit in church thinking about the tavern'. He was often accompanied by his colleague Philipp Melanchthon, who was also partial to a glass of beer, despite his ascetic reputation. (In fact, Melanchthon even had his own brewery in his later years, in true Wittenberg tradition.) Melanchthon was certainly no match for his friend as a drinker. Luther was said to have a large beer tankard at home with three decorative bands around it. He called the first one 'the Ten Commandments', the second 'the Creed' and the third 'the Lord's Prayer'. Whereas Luther could drain his tankard in one drink while going through the three pillars of faith in his head, he joked that Melanchthon could only get as far as the Commandments in his own theology of beer.

After the publication of his theses, Martin Luther was a public figure whose every movement was observed – and every pint counted. Luther's religious and political opponents frequently labelled him as a drunkard. However, nothing indicates that he was a large-scale consumer of alcohol. On the contrary: he preached moderation in his sermons. Food and drink were gifts from God, but they must not be misused. As an old man in 1544, Luther joked about drinking in his notes for a sermon on Noah: 'Tonight I intend to drink plenty so I can tell about that horrible event from my own experience.'

In 1525 Luther married Katharina von Bora, a former nun. Katharina had learned how to brew beer in her convent, and she continued brewing at home. However much Martin Luther liked the beers from Einbeck or Naumburg, he also appreciated the pale

Wittenberg beer brewed by his wife. But Katharina's beer was not the only thing the Luthers drank at their table. Ledgers preserved from the 1530s show that the Luther family spent 300 guldens per year on meat and 200 on buying beer. Bread accounted for 50 guldens of the household's spending.

Luther's enjoyment of beer has also been exaggerated over the years. Aphorisms such as this are attributed to him: 'He who drinks beer, is quick to sleep. He who sleeps long, does not sin. He who does not sin, shall enter heaven.' Framed reproductions of this saying are found on the walls of many drinking establishments in Germany, and you can even buy tankards emblazoned with it. It's a nice, logical thought sequence. However, there is not a single contemporary source indicating that Martin Luther ever said – or wrote – that aphorism. Another argument against its attribution is the fact that Luther consistently distinguished between freedom from sin and forgiveness. The requirement to enter heaven was not freedom from sin or intentional good deeds, but faith and the grace of God. In a letter to Melanchthon in 1521, Luther stated: 'Sin boldly, but believe and rejoice in Christ even more boldly.'

Although Luther preferred malty flavours to the fruit of the vine, he did not refuse to drink wine. There was also time for enjoyment in life. Nor is it known whether he ever uttered the saying he is famously credited with: 'He who loves not wine, women and song, remains a fool his whole life long.' The earliest documented user of that phrase was the German linguist Johann Heinrich Voss, who was born over two centuries later than Luther.

When Martin Luther died in 1546, the religious map of Europe was still in a state of flux. The dividing line between Protestants and Catholics in the Holy Roman Empire largely corresponded to the division between beer- and wine-drinking regions. Protestants dominated in the beer zone. They were in a strong position in northern and eastern Germany, including places like Bavaria, Bohemia and Silesia, which would later become

Catholic following the Thirty Years' War (1618–48). The Catholic Rhineland was wine territory. Outside the Holy Roman Empire, these links were less common. The Protestant teachings of John Calvin were popular in the wine-growing regions of southern France in the 16th century, while Scotland and Ireland, both beer-drinking nations, remained loyal to the Pope.

Later on, when the Thirty Years' War had cemented the denominational boundaries of Europe, we can identify some affinities between people's preferred tipples and their religious affiliations, though there are still some exceptions. Even today, beer-drinking Catholic countries include Ireland, Belgium and the Czech Republic, as well as the federal state of Bavaria in Germany. Wine-drinking areas with a Protestant majority include the French-speaking cantons of western Switzerland. It would be an exaggeration to say there is an exact match between Protestant regions and areas where beer is more commonly drunk than wine.

Some extra bite is lent to the story of religious schisms and beer by hops (*Humulus lupulus*), now an integral constituent of modern beers. In the same decades of the early 16th century when Europe began fighting over the principles of Christian teachings, the last major struggle was under way between gruit herbs and hops for the soul of beer.

Hops had been used to flavour beer since the 8th century, and especially so after *Physica*, a work written by the 12th-century scholar and mystic Hildegard of Bingen, made European learned circles aware of their use in brewing. 'Hops is a warm, dry plant that contains moderate moisture. [...] Its bitterness keeps some putrefactions from drinks so that they may last much longer.' Hildegard, later designated the patron saint of hops growers, also gives her own view on why hops are not widely used: 'It makes melancholy grow easily in man and makes the soul of man sad, and weighs down his inner organs.'

In those days, it was more common to use other herbs in

addition to hops to flavour beer. Gruit was a herb mixture that was especially popular. Its exact composition varied from one region to another, but the key elements were sweet gale (*Myrica gale*), which grows on bushes in bogs and along rivers and canals in central and northern Europe. Other common ingredients were rosemary, bay leaf, yarrow and spruce resin. Hildegard of Bingen was also familiar with gruit. She wrote of a plant called *Mirtelbaum*, which might mean bog myrtle – also found in Germany – rather than the myrtle bush (*Myrtus communis*) native to the Mediterranean coast: 'If one wants to make beer, he should cook the leaves and fruit of this plant with the beer. It will be good for the health and will not harm the one who drinks it.'

The benefits of gruit in brewing beer were quite similar to those of hops. Gruit gave the beer flavour, and above all it improved shelf life by making it bitter. Bog myrtle was commonly found in the lowlands of central Europe, so it was not difficult to get hold of gruit. It was not freely available, though. The earliest decrees granting monasteries the exclusive right to use gruit date back to the 9th century. This became a widespread practice throughout central Europe in the following centuries. Monasteries, bishoprics and other holders of gruit rights could also grant the right to use it to other brewers – for a fee. The sale of gruit rights became a sort of stealth tax on beer that generated significant revenue for the Catholic Church.

Hops were used as the main flavouring in beer in Poland, the Baltic countries and Russia in the 13th century. Gradually it challenged the supremacy of gruit in Germany and the Low Countries as well, but the change took centuries. On one hand there was the issue of maintaining old customs, but on the other, there was the bitter taste of hops. Beer flavoured with gruit was much sweeter than that made with hops. Hops won out over gruit in Holland in the 14th century, and in the 15th century the Church stopped collecting the gruit tax. The changeover occurred in Germany in the 15th and 16th centuries. Gruit remained in use longest of all in the Rhine region of western Germany. In Cologne for example, hops overtook gruit in popularity in the early 16th century. One by one, German breweries stopped using gruit, which gradually restricted the income of the Catholic Church. With the publication of Luther's theses, the switch from gruit to hops also became a political and a religious choice. There was no tax on hops to be paid to the pope, not even in Catholic-controlled regions. The popularity of gruit nosedived, and in a few decades in the early 16th century beer flavoured with bog myrtle became a relic of the past. The religious and brewing history of Europe had turned over a new, hops-flavoured leaf.

Einbecker Ur-Bock Dunkel

EINBECK, GERMANY

TYPE: bock
ABV: 6.5%
GRAVITY: 16.3°P
BITTERNESS: 36 EBU
COLOUR: 34 EBC

Martin Luther first tasted beer from Einbeck in 1521, when he defended his theses at the Diet of Worms. Four years later, when Luther celebrated his marriage to Katharina von Bora, he wanted to serve his guests 'the finest beer I know', as he himself described it. They ordered eleven tuns of beer – 4,400 litres – from Einbeck as part of the catering.

Brewing in Einbeck and other towns in northern Germany started to wane in the late 16th century, as the Hanseatic League was no longer exporting as much to other markets as before. The most famous master brewers relocated to Munich, where strong beer became known as 'bock' in the 17th century – derived from the Bavarian dialectal pronunciation of Einbeck as *Oanbock*, with the loss of the first syllable.

The Einbecker brewery maintained the brewing traditions of its hometown. Ur-Bock Dunkel is very similar to the renowned beer from the 16th century. It has a copper-brown colour and a sweet, malty aroma. It has a caramelly maltiness in the mouth, with a hint of spice, and leaves a well-balanced hoppy aftertaste.

A merry group in a Dutch tavern in the 17th century.
Adriaen Brouwer: The smokers, *1636.*

IV

Illustrators of peasants and taverns

For painters and other artists, beer has long been a source of inspiration – as a beverage as well as a subject matter. Depictions of beer flourished particularly in 16th- and 17th-century Dutch painting. Pieter Bruegel the Elder and Adriaen Brouwer have made their mark in art history with their beer-related themes. Their subjects are not the classic still lifes of a few pears, apples and a jug of beer; rather, these artists eloquently depicted the boisterous atmosphere of peasants' feasts and taverns.

Pieter Bruegel the Elder (1525–1569) was one of the greatest names of Flemish Renaissance art. He was born in the province of Limburg, on the border between present-day Belgium and the Netherlands, and studied painting in Antwerp. At the beginning of his career, Bruegel painted in Italy as well as Antwerp. He perfected his characteristic satirical style after relocating to Brussels in the early 1560s.

Even in his Antwerp period, Bruegel's paintings depicted the lives of peasants in the surrounding countryside. After his move to Brussels, even more of his paintings commemorated beer drinking. Unlike other Renaissance artists, Bruegel did not focus on people's more noble qualities. His works typically feature bleary-eyed, gawping simple folk, sometimes brawling, sometimes slouched on the ground, worn out from overconsumption of food or drink. His style of painting has provided art historians with plenty of food for thought. One common view is that Bruegel did not want to make fun of peasants the way many 'refined' paintings of his day did, but to skewer common human hypocrisy. The nobility who bought and admired Bruegel's paintings engaged in the very same vices as the common country folk depicted in them did – often without acknowledging their double standards. Thus the paintings served as a mirror of the soul of their observers.

While Bruegel does intentionally simplify his depictions of people, his paintings are considered to be very accurate portrayals of the customs and environment of the Brabantian countryside. Bruegel got to know the region of Pajottenland to the west of Brussels particularly well. Its hilly landscape can be seen in many of his paintings. The fertile Pajottenland produced food and drink for the markets and shops of Brussels. The region's most famous speciality is lambic beer brewed with wild yeasts in the Senne River valley, which Bruegel documents in his paintings on wooden panels.

In his painting *The Harvesters* (*De Oogst*, 1565) Bruegel depicts work and rest in the countryside. On the left side of the picture, farm workers toil in a hilly field, reaping wheat and tying it into sheaves. They are just juxtaposed with the workers taking their lunch break on the right. The latter group have bowls of rice pudding and are drinking beer from a large jug. One worker has decided to take a nap.

Beer is also evident in *The Peasant Wedding* (*De Boerenbruiloft*, 1568). An odd assortment of guests sit around a long table at a wedding party, where most people seem more interested in filling their bellies than talking to each other. The wealthy man at the head of the table remembers that man does not live by bread alone and is concentrating on saying grace, which the monk next to him disturbs with his chatter. Other guests at the feast are tucking into rice pudding or pouring beer down their gullets from earthenware jugs. In the background, the lower-status guests drink while standing up. A bagpipe player looks longingly at the food being brought out, and a servant fills jugs with pale beer. Art historians have detected allusions to the wedding at Cana: Bruegel is poking fun at his contemporaries for their self-centredness, the way they do not notice miracles going on around them.

There is a lively depiction of beer in Bruegel's *The Peasant Dance* (*De Boerendans*, 1568). Some peasants are kicking up their heels near a row of shops. Along with the dancing, a key component of the jolly atmosphere is its placement near a tavern, located on the left edge of the picture. The beer-drinkers gesticulate and offer the musician a drink. One tries to kiss his reluctant neighbour, while another urinates against the side of the tavern. The celebration appears to have been under way for quite some time, as a few drinkers are taking a little rest.

Bruegel married in 1563 and had two sons who also became painters: Pieter (known as Pieter Bruegel the Younger) was born in 1564 and Jan in 1568. Relatively little is known about the life of Bruegel the Elder, when you consider that he was a respected artist during his own lifetime. The cause of his early death (in 1569 at the age of 44) was not been recorded.

Although Brueghel's own beer preferences remain shrouded in history, plenty of anecdotes have been passed down the generations about the drinking habits of another Flemish master, Adriaen Brouwer. Even his name provides an omen: *brouwer* means 'brewer' in Dutch. However, it is also possible that his surname came not from his family's occupation but from their origins in La Bruyère in north-western France.

Brouwer was born in the town of Oudenaarde in Flanders in

1606. He left home at the age of 16, heading for the limitless opportunities of Amsterdam to embark on life as an artist. He quickly gained a reputation not only as a talented painter but also as a regular customer in the alehouses of Amsterdam and Haarlem. There were plenty of buyers for Brouwer's works, and he was aware of his worth. He earned good money from his paintings, but because of his lifestyle he was constantly in debt. His epitaph by Cornelius de Bie stated: 'He painted slowly, and could spend like the best, / and in low piss-pot taverns smoked and drank with zest'.

Those cheap, dirty 'piss-pot taverns' were also where Brouwer found his subject matter. Moving to Antwerp in his native region in 1631 did not change anything. His debts continued to dog him, and taverns continued to be his second home. Brawls, card games, pipe smoking and beer drinking constituted his core themes. Sometimes Brouwer would depict country pubs, other times city taverns. The interiors of these drinking establishments had the same dark wood that can still be seen in 'brown bars' in the Netherlands. There are many dark things depicted in Brouwer's paintings, including the beer. In most cases this was probably Flanders brown ale, *oud bruin*. Today the Brouwerij Roman brewery in Brouwer's hometown of Oudenaarde brews a beer it sells under the name of Adriaen Brouwer – appropriately enough, it is a brown ale.

Brouwer's art displays an interesting tension between his coarse subjects and his refined painting technique. People's expressions are the focus of his tavern paintings in dark shades. For example, in *The Smokers* (*Mannen roken*, 1636) one man jauntily raises his tankard while another puts a finger to the side of his nose, a third smiles to himself and a couple of others concentrate on blowing smoke rings. Meanwhile, a glass of brown beer has pride of place among the drinkers around a table in *In the Tavern* (*In de taverne*, 1630s).

Art exacts a heavy toll. Brouwer's heart, weakened by his incessant smoking, heavy drinking and poor diet, gave out in 1638 when he was just 31 years old. Penniless, he was buried first in a mass grave, but the members of the artists' guild later arranged for a final resting place for Brouwer's remains in the Carmelite monastery in Antwerp. The cause of death stated on his gravestone is not a heart attack but simply 'poverty'.

Not all tavern painters died before their time, though. Besides Bruegel and Brouwer, two more painters known for their beer-themed works are David Teniers the Younger (1610–1690) and Adriaen van Ostade (1610–1685). These four artists laid the foundations for Dutch genre painting, which took its themes from everyday life.

The works by Teniers, a Flemish painter, are like a combination of Brouwer and Brueghel's beer themes. Sometimes he painted tavern scenes in dark hues, like the pensive *Smoker Leaning his Elbow on a Table* (*Roker scheve zijn elleboog op een tafel*, 1643). Other paintings feature lush colours, with beer-refreshed peasants dancing enthusiastically, as in Bruegel's works. Van Ostade, a Dutchman, liked to portray people drinking beer in everyday life. One of his best-known works is *The Violinist* (*Violist voor een boerderij*, 1673).

These four painters all share a precise attention to detail in their oil paintings. In comparing their works, one can discern differences in the beer culture in different parts of the Low Countries. Darker beer varieties were preferred in Holland around Amsterdam and in Flanders near Antwerp, while in Brussels and Brabant people often drank lighter lambics and wheat beers. A general increase in prosperity can also be seen. Bruegel's 16th-century peasants drank from simple earthenware jugs. In the next century, even rural pubs had mugs with handles. Wooden tankards with lids were seen in city taverns. In more middle-class establishments, people had started using fluted beer glasses, which

David Teniers the Younger also emphasises in his painting *Self-Portrait in a Tavern* (*Zelfportret in de taverne*, 1646). Judging by his languid, satisfied expression, life as an artist could taste very good indeed.

Lindemans Faro

VLEZENBEEK, BELGIUM

TYPE: lambic
ABV: 4.5%
GRAVITY: 16°P
BITTERNESS: 23 EBU
COLOUR: 25 EBC

Lambic beers can be drunk just as they are after barrel fermentation. Usually, though, raw lambics are used as the base for blends of matured and freshly brewed beers (known as *gueuze*), various fruit beers or *faro*. Faro is a blend of barrel-fermented and one-year-matured lambics and candy sugar. This makes faro more accessible than gueuze and gives it its characteristic fresh taste: a balance of sweetness and acidity.

In paintings by Brueghel and Teniers, peasants in the countryside near Brussels are depicted drinking cloudy pale beer (probably gueuze) as well as slightly darker lambic, with a colour indicative of faro. In the 17th century lambic and wheat beers were typically served in narrow fluted glasses as seen in many paintings by Teniers and van Ostade.

Vlezenbeek, a small town of 3,000 on the outskirts of Brussels, is a culinary powerhouse. It is home to the renowned Neuhaus chocolatier as well as the family-owned Lindemans brewery, founded in 1822, which is one of nine authentic lambic breweries in Belgium. Lindemans Faro is a sparkling, amber-coloured lambic beer with a hint of candy sugar. It has a well-balanced flavour and an understated tartness.

An encounter between a soldier and a peasant.
Copperplate print from the Thirty Years' War.

A victory powered by Ur-Krostitzer

The Free State of Saxony (in German, *Freistaat Sachsen*), located in central Germany on the Czech border, was known during the time of the Holy Roman Empire as the Electorate of Saxony but is now one of the federal states of Germany. Its major cities are Leipzig and Dresden. North of Leipzig is the town of Krostitz, whose neighbouring village of Breitenfeld became famous for two battles (in 1631 and 1642) during the Thirty Years' War in which Swedish artillerymen and even Finnish dragoons distinguished themselves. Like many other German villages and towns, Krostitz has feudal origins. According to popular legend, the Elector of Saxony granted one of his loyal knights an estate, along with its serfs, north of Leipzig. It is not known for certain whether the knight took his title of von Crostewitz from the estate or whether the estate and then also the village were named Crostewitz (later shortened to Krostitz) after their lord. However it happened, Crostewitz/Crostitz/Krostitz (the spelling varied) was known for its beer and hops in the Middle Ages, and its brewing tradition has links to no less a personage than King Gustavus Adolphus of Sweden from the time of the Thirty Years' War (1618–1648). These days Krostitz is part of greater Leipzig and travellers might drive through the suburb without paying it much notice, if it weren't for the smell of the brewery.

In the early stages of the Thirty Years' War, John George I, Elector of Saxony, favoured the imperial Habsburgs and the Catholic faith, and his electorate was not significantly affected by the fighting in the war. That situation changed when he joined an alliance with the Swedes in 1630 after they had entered the war. He also switched his allegiance to Protestantism. The ravages of war now spread over Saxony as well.

In those days many more soldiers succumbed to disease, especially intestinal infections, than to enemy weapons, and disease also wiped out many civilians left behind after battles. One of the most significant sources of infection was contaminated drinking water. While many brands of mineral water sold in bottles at good prices all over Europe have excellent reputations, and today's supermarkets devote enormous shelf space to water, this has a tradition of its own as well.

Just think of a typical European city block, surrounded on all four sides by buildings of several storeys, with their façades facing the street. In the middle of the block, in between all the houses, was a courtyard with woodsheds, outdoor privies and stalls for horses and other animals around it. In the middle was a well. Hundreds of people lived in this setting, along with the horses, pigs, chickens, rabbits and other livestock they used for transport and food. It doesn't take much imagination to understand how mucky the well water was in cities in past times, with none of the water and sewer networks we have today.

Conditions were much the same in the countryside. Even where well water in villages and estates was not an immediate health risk, it did not taste good after hundreds of years of human settlement. Stomach illnesses were common, and even recently it was usual to accuse Jews or other scapegoated groups of poisoning the well.

A regular side-effect of wars and unrest was the contamination of wells. With large numbers of men and horses on the move, they left droppings behind, and soldiers advancing or retreating through enemy territory had other things on their mind than hygiene.

Through the ages, brewers have emphasised the importance of clean water. Even slight impurities which only a modern chemist in a laboratory or an expert taster from Mouton-Rothschild could detect in well water or spring water can give a distinct, easily noticeable tinge to the taste of beer. The purer the water a brewer uses to brew his beer, the easier he can sell it. When wort was still cooked according to standard practice and then left to ferment in thoroughly clean vessels where the bittering substances in hops and the resulting alcohol inhibited bacteria growth, beer was safe to drink – it was virtually sterile, compared to the water that was available. In times gone by, when people knew nothing about bacteria or other microbes, they noticed that beer drinkers stayed healthier than people who stuck to drinking water. No wonder, then, that troop movement and battle strategies also took the availability of beer in the local area into account.

It would be an overstatement to claim that battle plans were drawn up solely on the basis of the availability of beer. However, it is true that when troops entered a settlement, they gave the available water to their horses and satisfied their own needs for liquid from taverns and breweries first. When they had exhausted those supplies, they helped themselves to the cellars of peasants' hovels and city homes. They moved on to water only after they had drunk all the sources of beer dry. There are many accounts from all over Germany of the misery inflicted on the land and its inhabitants by troops' requisitions during the Thirty Years' War. For example, in 1632–33 the residents of Leipzig complained at the way the advancing and retreating troops had expropriated everything, leaving barely enough straw to feed the cattle, while they had to make bread from whatever they could find, even pea pods and grain husks, and there was no beer to be had whatsoever.

Harvest time has always been a time for farmers to celebrate – especially when the harvest is good. The term *Erntebier*, or 'harvest beer', is well known in Germany. It has a variety of meanings. It primarily refers to beer brewed in late summer, which is drunk young and frothy to celebrate the autumn grain harvest. It could also refer to a beer brewed quickly from the bounty of the land – besides the malt, this could even include pears, carrots and honey! – in good times to communicate the abundance of the new harvest, and in straitened times to have something festive on the table. And as modern-day Oktoberfest visitors know, 'harvest beer' can also refer to a skilfully fermented, matured, full-bodied beer brewed from the previous year's grain harvest, drunk to symbolically finish off last year's crop in celebration of the new one. It is worth noting that in 1671, with reference to the Reinheitsgebot, or purity law, Saxony outlawed the use of the word 'beer' to refer to malt beverages that had been supplemented with fruits or vegetables as described above. The ban was renewed in 1703.

In the summer of 1631 the war had progressed through Leipzig and its environs. With the arrival of autumn, retreating Catholic troops led by the Count of Tilly seized all the foodstuffs they came across, including grain that had been harvested but not yet threshed. Infectious diseases such as the dreaded plague had already begun to spread. There were some fields where the crops had been left unharvested, and with winter approaching, local residents placed their hopes in them.

Soon after the Catholics had passed through Krostitz, Swedish Protestant troops marched in. Legend has it that they prompted great admiration: tall, handsome, well-equipped and disciplined soldiers who asked for things rather than stole them, and paid hard cash for the things they received.

On the morning of the 17th of September, an unnamed

landowner was left waiting for his hired men, who had gone to bring in the season's last load of wheat sheaves. There was no sign of the men, much less the loaded carts, and the landowner feared the worst: what could have happened to them? Had they been ambushed by the enemy?

The load of grain was nowhere to be seen.

In the distance on the main country road, he saw a solitary man on horseback trotting lively. With ice in his heart, the landowner saw that the horseman had noticed him. Was it going to be something new his men would be blamed for, and what would happen to his harvest beer which he had managed to keep hidden in his cellar? From where he stood, he wouldn't even be able to escape through the gate.

The horseman stopped with his steaming horse in front of the landowner by the gate. The landowner sized up the man: his horse was a purebred, and the rider had a noble, ruddy-cheeked look about him. He wore the clothes of a nobleman. The stranger opened the conversation with a polite enquiry: 'Have you any brewing equipment in this house?' The landowner was unable to deny it. 'Are you the landowner?' Again he grunted a brief answer in the affirmative. 'Have you any beer?'

The landowner felt the coldness spreading from his heart into his entire being. Denying it now would just make matters worse, because the truth would become clear anyway, for better or worse. So he formulated his reply carefully: 'Only a very little, what I have reserved for my harvest beer.' 'Thanks be to God, that is wonderful! On behalf of the King of Sweden, who will soon be passing this way, I seek a bit of refreshment for His Majesty. On the journey, you see, everything has been drunk, even the water. In His Majesty's name I now ask of you: take your finest jug and fill it to the brim with beer and set off on that road, ready to greet the monarch with due respect.'

Having delivered this message, the courtier, who according

to the story was 17-year-old August von Leubelfing, turned his horse round and rode off towards the main road. The landowner, relieved that it was in fact the Swedes, and that he had been deemed worthy of performing a service for the mighty king, soon went off in the same direction with a full jug of beer.

The noble party approached. Ranks of dusty infantrymen were followed by half a squadron of dragoons, and then under the blue-and-yellow flag a group of cavalrymen. The landowner recognised the king of Sweden among them. The king exclaimed: 'Ah, look, a Good Samaritan who will quench my thirst!' He halted his horse and took the jug held out by the landowner. Briefly overcome by the grandeur of the situation, the landowner launched into verse: 'May Your Majesty drink his fill / and may the enemy fall to his will!'

The king laughed and replied: 'Now I have no choice but to drink every last drop.' Then he drank the beer in big gulps, wiped his beard and said: 'That hit the spot. Beer like this is strong, flavourful and worthy of its reputation! May the Lord reward you for this good deed you did for the allies of your land. And take this with my thanks.' As he said that, the king took a gold ring set with a large ruby off his finger and placed it in the jug he had drained, then returned it to the landowner. Then the king and his entourage rode off towards Breitenfeld.

Around midday the sounds of artillery fire started coming from the direction of Breitenfeld, and when the din of battle subsided in the afternoon confirmation arrived of the Swedes' great victory.

The story does not say what happened to the load of grain and the men who went to fetch it, or what sort of harvest festival the unnamed landowner celebrated. But the well from which the water was drawn to make such excellent beer came to be called the *Schwedenquelle*, or 'Swedish well'. People in Krostitz still say that the Protestant victory in Breitenfeld was thanks to the excellent beer that reinvigorated a thirsty King Gustavus Adolphus as he rode into battle on the 17th of September 1631.

Back to reality now. The first definite mention of Rittergut Crostewitz, or Crostewitz Manor, dates from 1349, when it was part of the property the Elector of Saxony granted as fiefs. The parcel of land included a brewery – it is in Germany, after all. Its beer had an excellent reputation right from the start, and it is said that Krostitz beer was praised by Martin Luther himself. There is no contemporary source to corroborate the story about Gustavus Adolphus, though. In modern-day terms, it might have been a marketing tactic to create a brand in Saxony which remained Protestant after the religious war. Whatever the truth of the matter, the story has been used in marketing Krostitz beer since the time of the Thirty Years' War, and the treasures held by the brewery still include an 'exact copy' of the king's ring. The beer is still brewed with water sourced from the *Schwedenquelle*. True, the well collapsed into the sandy local soil long ago, but today's brewery still uses the same water from the underground aquifer. It should also be mentioned that in the German version of the story, the king uses the word *würzig*, which literally means 'worty', indicating that they did not skimp on the malt or the hops when making the wort. A beer like this also gains authority from its alcohol content, left to mature in the cellar.

In the 17th century the brewery remained primarily a local enterprise, due to the transport conditions alone. Slow but significant progress was made over the following century or so. People began building wide, hard-surfaced roads that heavy loads of grain and beer could travel over more easily, and then the railroad came in the 19th century. Improved transport links opened up new avenues for entrepreneurial owners and master brewers to streamline their production, increase distribution and create a brand. The same happened in Krostitz. The former *Rittergut* was acquired by one Heinrich Oberländer in 1803, who established the Oberländer brewing dynasty, which lasted for over 120 years. The brewery was spun off into a separate company in 1878, and in 1907 it became a limited company by the name of *Aktiengesellschaft Bierbrauerei Klein-Crostitz F. Oberländer AG*. By the mid-19th century the number of employees at the brewery had increased from around 40 to over 200, and the former wooden building had been replaced by a complex of five-storey stone buildings covering an entire block. Krostitz beer was known throughout central Germany.

When Germany was divided after the Second World War, Leipzig and the Krostitz brewery ended up in East Germany. The former Oberländer company became VEB Brauerei Krostitz (the abbreviation stands for *Volkseigener Betrieb*, or 'People's Enterprise') and the only note of bourgeois levity that was retained in the socialist workers' paradise was a stylised portrait of King Gustavus Adolphus on the labels on the bottles.

Ur-Krostitzer Feinherbes Pilsner

KROSTITZ, GERMANY

TYPE: pilsener
ABV: 4.9%
GRAVITY: 11.7°P
BITTERNESS: 26 EBU
COLOUR: 8 EBC

Since German reunification in 1990 the Krostitz brewery, now operating under the name Krostitzer Brauerei, has been a part of the Radeberger Gruppe brewing corporation. The brewery still maintains its Swedish connections: labels on its bottles feature a portrait of Sweden's King Gustavus Adolphus, now with a sterner expression than before. The brewery also has its own heritage committee which re-enacts scenes from the Thirty Years' War in period Swedish costumes on special occasions. The plant even has a museum and memorial hall dedicated to Gustavus Adolphus, and the current king and queen of Sweden have paid a visit.

The brewery was completely rebuilt in the early 21st century and is one of the most modern such facilities in Europe. It produces around 400,000 hectolitres of beer annually, watched over by the stern countenance of Gustavus Adolphus. These days its leading product is its Feinherbes Pilsner, a pleasantly bitter pilsener with aromas of herbs, hops and apple. Its flavour is dry, malty and slightly sweet.

Peter the Great visited the London docks in 1698. That was where he also encountered porter, as drunk by the workers.
Peter Maclise: Peter the Great at Deptford Dockyard, *1857.*

VI

A thirst for Europeanness in Russia

Peter the Great stood head and shoulders above other men – not just in terms of his height (203 cm or 6' 8"), but also his personal characteristics. On the battlefield he was the bravest of the brave; as a statesman he was the most far-sighted of all, and at booze-ups he had the greatest thirst. He regularly drank enough vodka to kill less experienced drinkers. Unfortunately the Russian people were also keen drinkers, but most did not have Peter's tolerance for liquor. Peter understood the problem and decided it was time for the people to dry out. He turned his gaze westwards in search of a solution to Mother Russia's craving for booze.

Peter had become the titular ruler of Russia in 1682 at the age of 10, together with his severely disabled half-brother Ivan V. In practice, Peter's half-sister Sophia and his mother Natalia ruled as regents until Peter reached the age of majority. The future tsar did not need to worry his head with day-to-day matters of government, so he could concentrate on learning a wide range of life skills in his youth.

One of Peter's passions was Europe. At the end of the 17th century Russia was a backward country, still living in a sort of Dark Age. Opportunities for work were inflexible, people did not welcome innovations and the church had a central role in society. Young Peter's advisers, Patrick Gordon from Scotland and Franz Lefort from Switzerland, told him exciting tales of rapid advances in the West. Gordon was familiar with the education systems and armies of Europe, while Lefort knew a few things about commerce, seafaring and the good things in life. Lefort's drinking tales made a great impression on Peter. Whereas the Russians seemed to drink vodka primarily in order to pass out, Lefort just got more animated and talkative when he was tipsy.

At around the age of 17 or 18, Peter started to get a reputation for himself in Moscow's nightlife. Thanks to his enormous size – and with increasing experience – he was able to drink more than anyone else. His unofficial club, the All-Joking, All-Drunken Synod of Fools and Jesters, became particularly well known as their carousing could last for several days. The clergy frowned on the group's unruly behaviour, but many bishops and monks were flattered to be invited along to the group's sloshed 'synods'.

After Peter had taken up his position as Tsar in the early 1690s and fought against the Ottomans for control of the Sea of Azov (and onward to the Black Sea) in 1695, he embarked on a grand tour to gather practical experience of what it was to be European. The primary objective of his trip was to modernise the Russian army and commission the building of naval ships, but Peter also wanted to modernise Russia more generally – even extending to its meals.

After enjoying themselves in the Low Countries, Peter and his entourage arrived in London in January 1698. He took an apartment above a pub in Norfolk Street (now Temple Place) right on the Thames. Peter would go down to the docks every day to observe the workings of the harbour, and he even pitched in and did some work with his own hands. Then, after work, it was time for evening activities. The Russians sampled the dark beers favoured by the dock workers in the pub downstairs. According to a contemporary account, a barmaid was filling a tankard for Peter when the tsar, laughing, stopped her and said, 'Forget the mug! Give me a jug!' When they weren't drinking beer and smoking pipes, the men also enjoyed brandy. Later in the spring, when the Russians had secured private lodgings near the Deptford Docks, beer gave way to working men's drinks. They completely trashed the house, which was owned by the author John Evelyn. He had to replace the floors on three storeys and basically all the furniture and fittings. Accounting ledgers state that the Russians paid for repairs to items including fifty chairs smashed for firewood, twenty paintings slashed, three hundred window-panes broken and all the locks in the house destroyed.

Nevertheless, in August 1698 Peter returned to Russia a ruler full of enthusiasm, declaring it was time for the Russian people to dry out and cheer up. Peter himself opted for just the cheering up part. He implemented his military innovations and, in the space of just a few years, gained enemies in every direction. In 1703 he decreed that the Peter and Paul Fortress should be built on the Neva River delta, conquered from Sweden. That building project gave him an appetite for more. Just a year later, he decided to make the city of St Petersburg, still under construction, the capital of the Russian Empire.

Of course, building is also thirsty work. Peter the Great made particularly sure that the work stayed on course and so the workmen were given beer to drink. The harbour lads and dock workers in London had drunk the same dark elixir and there had been no evidence of laziness or drunkenness – except maybe among the Russian visitors. The architects and master builders of the future capital were served the same beer shipped in from England that the Tsar drank in his palace. The workmen had to settle for beers brewed locally, but they were not too bad either. Russia did have a centuries-long brewing history, after all.

Prince Vladimir of Kiev, who would also later gain the

appellation 'the Great', had spent a great deal of time in the late 10th century musing on which religion to choose for himself and his people. The story goes that he ruled out Islam because it forbids alcohol. Finally, Vladimir chose Byzantium over Rome and opened Russia's doors to Orthodox Christianity. One aspect of the legend worth mentioning here is that Russia has not always been a vodka-drinking country, despite its formidable reputation. Russians did not become familiar with distilled liquor until half a millennium later, so when Vladimir rejected Islam for his people in the 10th century, he was thinking of other drinks: mead, *kvas* (a drink made from fermented rye or bread) and beer. The Russian word хмель (*hmel*) refers to both the hops plant (*Humulus lupulus*) used to flavour beer and the intoxicating effect of alcohol. This dual meaning also indicates the primary role of beer as the drink that made Russians drunk. Habits changed later on, though. The earliest written mention of distilling vodka in Russia dates from 1558. By the end of that same century, people were complaining that hard liquor had become a national problem.

Beer made a comeback in the era of Peter the Great. Particularly in the middle and upper classes in the cities – which also happened to be the most Westernised segments of society – people started to prefer beer and other 'European' drinks to vodka. Poor people in rural areas traditionally drank mead. This switch was short-lived, however. The west winds died down as Peter grew older, and getting the population to dry out was no longer considered a key issue. Vodka had its good points, too: it brought plenty of taxes into the state coffers.

The decades following the reign of Peter the Great were marked by recurring palace coups. Members of the imperial court continued to drink beer, but French drinks ranging from wine to cognac were more in vogue. Beer came back into fashion in the 1760s, when German-born Catherine the Great enjoyed malt beverages. Her father had sent a consignment of Saxon beer for her wedding in the city of Zerbst. Catherine did not really like the taste of Russian beers after her years in Germany. Every year she placed an enormous order for strong, dark beer to be sent to the court from London. She also urged Russian breweries to employ English master brewers. They followed her advice, and the quality of beer was said to improve.

As Russia's beer production was reformed, sales flourished. Beer imports soared during Catherine's long reign (1762–1796). In 1784 the English travel writer William Coxe recalled his visit to St Petersburg: '. . .I never tasted English beer and porter in greater perfection and abundance.' From 1793 to 1795 beer imports totalled half a million roubles in value, in monetary terms around twice as much as the amount of imported spices. Catherine had still not managed to change the course of Russia's drinking habits. Vodka consumption increased by a factor of 2.5 in the 18th century – and the trend carried on. Since the 1990s, though, beer has become increasingly popular in Russia. Once again, it is associated with images of Europeanness. Educated urbanites have been the keenest to switch from vodka to beer.

While women are underrepresented everywhere in historical accounts, the annals of beer history seem to be exceptionally male-dominated. Catherine the Great, who boasted she could match the men of the imperial court at drinking beer, serves as a refreshing exception. Many women, such as the beer widows of Tartu mentioned in the next chapter, have remained nameless figures on the sidelines of history. Few notable women of past centuries are known as beer aficionados, with the possible exception of Empress Elisabeth of Austria, known as Sissi.

There is a wide range of beers named after great men of history. We have selected a few representative examples for this book. Beers named after great women are rarer. However, the Smisje brewery in Belgium named its imperial stout after Catherine the Great. Baroness Ulrike von Levetzow of Bohemia (1804–1899) has her own namesake beer (Žatec Baronka). In 1822 the German author Johann Wolfgang von Goethe went on holiday in the mountains of Bohemia, where he met 18-year-old Ulrike. The young noble girl guided the 73-year-old writer around the area to show him the sights, and they also stopped off at a local brewery. The Bohemian beer, made with noble hops, and the young lady's beauty enthralled the old man. After he returned home, Goethe could not get the young baroness out of his mind and seriously considered asking her to marry him. The romance never led to a relationship, but it did result in some of Goethe's finest, most personal poems, such as the Marienbad Elegy.

Baltika №6 Porter

ST PETERSBURG, RUSSIA

TYPE: porter
ABV: **7.0%**
GRAVITY: **15.5°P**
BITTERNESS: **23 EBU**
COLOUR: **162 EBC**

The Russian imperial court enjoyed drinking very strong stout beers shipped over from England. Later on, in the 19th century, these started to be called 'imperial stout'. Baltic porters came about when breweries in St Petersburg and its environs began brewing similar dark beers in the 18th century. This type of beer goes well with traditional Russian *zakuska* cold dishes, such as rye bread and pickled cucumbers.

The brewing traditions were maintained even through the Soviet era, even though the quality of the end product varied. A brand-new brewery, intended to rescue the reputation of Soviet beer, was planned for Leningrad. It was completed in 1990, when the USSR was already in its death throes. The Baltica Brewery was privatised in 1992, and within four years the company grew to become Russia's largest producer of beer. Owned by Carlsberg since 2008, it is now the second-largest brewer in Europe.

Baltika №6 Porter is a cold-fermented brewer's yeast beer, unlike its British predecessors. It is nearly black in colour and forms a dense white head when poured into a glass. It has aromas of rye bread, toastiness and dark fruits. Its taste is somewhat dry and evokes rye and a hint of chocolate, and there are notes of orange and hops in the aftertaste.

Women and children were usually restricted to lowly roles in breweries, but in 18th-century Tartu they were given overall responsibility for all the brewing in the city.
17th-century woodcut.

VII

A safety net for orphans

From the end of the Middle Ages, the activity of brewing beer in major European cities began to be concentrated exclusively within guilds. This was also true in Tartu, Estonia, one of the oldest cities in northern Europe. For centuries, only members of a large guild were allowed to brew beer in that city. In the 18th century, a smaller guild challenged that monopoly. The Russian authorities, growing impatient with the dispute between the guilds, utilised the wisdom of Solomon and decreed in 1783 as part of a wide-ranging government reform that neither guild should control the sale of beer. From then on, beer would be brewed in Tartu by widows, orphans and other persons with no other means of supporting themselves.

In Britain and the Netherlands, brewery guild systems got their start back in the 14th century. Originally their purpose was to secure their members' livelihoods. As no increase in the number of breweries was desired, that meant there were two ways of becoming a member of the guild: by either inheriting or purchasing a brewery. The skills required varied from city to city. For example, in 15th-century Wismar in Germany the guild regulations stated that a brewery could be purchased by any upstanding man of the city. No previous brewing experience was necessary. Anyone seeking to become a master brewer in Munich had to prove he had at least two years' experience under his belt. In Paris, the guild required no less than five years' experience before they would deign to grant a permit to own a brewery.

The guild system also helped in ensuring the quality of beer. When new competitors could not enter the field without the approval of the guild, master brewers could spend more time on refinements to their brewing without needing to undercut on price. Often master brewers selected a tester from among their numbers to be in overall charge of quality monitoring for several years. The tester had unhindered access to every brewery, where he could inspect the ingredients, monitor the processes and taste the results. If he detected any shortcomings, the consequences ranged from warnings to fines and, at the most severe, expulsion from the guild – in other words, essentially losing the brewery. One sign of the high esteem in which the guild's internal system of controls was held was the tradition in Ghent of never locking brewery doors. Beer was what kept the city running, so it was important to look after its quality.

The guilds' practices spread throughout the Baltic region in the 15th century thanks to the network of Hanseatic cities. The earliest mention of a major guild brewing permit in Tartu dates from 1461, but references to brewing beer have been found from around the time that city was founded in the 13th century. Unlike in central Europe, there was no separate brewers' guild in Tartu; instead, the brewery owners belonged to the same large guild as other merchants. Its members were exclusively German-speaking. A smaller guild, whose members were more middle-class crafts-men, included both German and Estonian speakers.

Power changed hands several times from the mid-16th century onwards, following the decline of the Livonian Order, an auton-omous branch of the Teutonic Order. Tartu came under Russian control in 1558, then was ceded to Poland in 1582 and later to Sweden in 1625. Its new rulers did not rescind the traditional rights concerning brewing; rather, they added their own amendments to the regulations. For example, in 1582 the Polish king Stefan Batory decreed that only the city's taverns could sell beer within a 10-km radius of the centre of Tartu.

Tartu was destroyed by fire in 1708 during the Great Northern War, and it took a long time before the city was back on its feet. In 1717, well before the official end of the war, the Russian Tsar Peter the Great announced that the privileges for brewing and selling beer in Tartu were still in force. The smaller guild did not accept that state of affairs, though. The city was under Russian occupation and there was no new permanent government, so some guild members tried their luck and started brewing beer. Arguments – even fisticuffs – broke out between the guilds, but the interim government did not step in. Not even the Treaty of Nystad in 1721, when Tartu officially became part of the Russian Empire, solved the dispute. That same year, Peter's College of Justice issued an ambiguous judgment which did not take an explicit stand on the jurisdictions of the various guilds. A decades-long period of complaints and disputes ensued.

Finally in 1782 the College of Justice admitted there was no justification for the guilds' brewing privileges. However, brewing was not deregulated; instead, the exclusive right was transferred elsewhere. Empress Catherine the Great decreed that a brewery corporation should be founded in Tartu to handle all beer brewing in the city. The Governor-General of Livonia, an Irishman named George von Browne, was in charge of the practical organisation, using as its model a brewery founded a couple of decades previously in Riga.

The Tartu brewing company (in German: *Dorpater Brauer-Compagnie*, using the German-language name for Tartu, *Dorpat*) not only ended the beer battles between the guilds but also did its part to look after the upkeep of the poor. It only accepted as members widows from families who had been part of the guilds, as well as orphans and guild members who had become impoverished through no fault of their own. Members of the company were both employees and shareholders, and thus the company was able to ensure a livelihood for guild family members who had no other occupation. To prevent the brewery company from becoming a battleground between the guilds, it was decreed that its membership should equal that of the large and small guild combined.

With the passing decades Tartu had recovered from the numerous fires of the Great Northern War. The city had just under 4,000 thirsty residents. Food was preserved by salting and drying, which contributed to the demand for beverages. Consumption in the 18th century was impressive by modern standards. Documents from Tartu at the beginning of the century give a daily figure for each man and woman in the city of one jug of beer: 2.6 litres. Soldiers were to be given a jug and a half of drink, and on Sundays the faithful should have two whole jugs of the frothy stuff to enjoy. A large proportion of this was probably home-brewed beer or malt beverage. In the 1780s the brewing corporation produced up to 200 litres of beer per city inhabitant each year, over half a litre a day.

The brewing corporation seemed to be off to a flying start. It obtained a loan from the city to erect a larger brewery on the bank of the Ema river, a stone's throw from the guildhall. Besides brewing, the company held a monopoly on operating taverns in the city environs. The company was not involved in their day-to-day running; rather, it received income from granting pub permits and from the sale of beer. It is estimated there were around sixty alehouses in Tartu in the latter half of the 18th century.

The brewing company's structure was largely similar to that of a modern-day cooperative. Its aim was not to maximise profits but to provide a living for its members. The company was managed by two aldermen, one appointed by each of the guilds. It paid a wage to its members who brewed and distributed beer. If there was anything left over after other costs, loan amortisation and taxes had been paid, it was divided among the members. If a member wished to leave the company and take up other work, a corresponding amount was paid out for their share in the company. A new member was sought to take their place, and deductions would be made from his wages for the first few years to pay for his share.

In the late 18th century, impecunious citizens of Riga, Pärnu and Tallinn were also in charge of brewing beer in those cities. Though historical records do not show evidence of other cooperative enterprises like the Baltic brewery companies, women have a presence in brewery history. In Estonia as elsewhere in Europe, women had commonly brewed beer for home consumption. It was not unusual for brewers' widows to carry on the business after the death of their husbands. There are also examples of independent unmarried women who became brewers in medieval and early modern Europe. These female entrepreneurs do not seem to have received equal treatment, however. In Munich, an appeal was made to the city authorities in 1599 to withdraw a brewing permit from the widow of a master brewer, because 'women are not capable of learning the precious skill of brewing beer'. The appeal did not result in action, so women were allowed to continue owning Bavarian breweries. In England, drink brewed by 'alewives' was often criticised for being of poor quality. British moral guardians were also horrified by female publicans who lured menfolk onto the path of drunkenness.

Problems emerged in Tartu as well. After its first years of operation, the brewery's sales began to decline. The quality of its beer was criticised, and the more refined segments of the city began purchasing more and more of their drink from rural breweries. The rural nobility had had a hereditary right to brew beer from the days of Polish rule. Although rurally produced beer could not be sold in Tartu or its environs, there were a number of estate breweries within a 20–30 km radius where the city's burghers could obtain their drink. The brewing company's widows were left penniless and the city was deprived of tax revenues. Many Tartu taverns, bowing to their customers' preferences, started to shun the beer from the brewing company, and since they were not permitted to sell any other malt beverage, the pubs switched to selling vodka.

Emperor Paul I succeeded to the Russian throne in 1796. He set about reforming the government of Livonia and the other Baltic territories, largely overturning the reforms his mother, Catherine the Great, had instituted in 1783. The council of Tartu spotted an opportunity to extricate itself from the brewery company it had been operating in the city for over a decade.

No one suggested directly that widows and orphans would be abandoned, so the city would not have to lose out on tax revenues and the residents of Tartu could have better-quality beer to drink. The solution developed was to lease brewing rights – the same way the rights to operate taverns had been handled previously. The brewing company still had a nominal exclusive right to carry on brewing activities, but it could grant operating permits to private companies. The business model worked. Numerous private breweries were set up in the city, and everyone was satisfied with the beer. The income from leases provided basic security for orphans, who were freed from brewing to look for work on the free market. The system clearly seemed to be working – at least there were no reports of impoverished people who starved as a result of the reorganisation. Beer money continued to flow through the brewing company as social security for poor residents until 1820.

A. Le Coq Porter

TARTU, ESTONIA

TYPE: porter
ABV: 6.5 %
GRAVITY: 14.6 °P
BITTERNESS: 17 EBU
COLOUR: 64 EBC

Albert Le Coq founded a company bearing his name in London in 1807 to trade in wine and beer. One of his most popular products was a strong dark ale which the A. Le Coq company exported from London breweries to the Russian market. In 1974 Norwegian divers discovered the wreck of the Olivia, a steamship which had sunk in the Baltic in 1869. Its cargo included A. Le Coq porter bound for Russia.

Tariffs protecting Russia's domestic beer production led the company to expand its operations in St Petersburg in the early 20th century. In 1912 A. Le Coq & Co purchased the Tivoli brewery in Tartu and began producing porter within the borders of the Russian empire. That same year A. Le Coq was designated an official supplier to the Imperial court. The Le Coq brewery was under state ownership during the period of Soviet occupation, but it was privatised when Estonia gained its independence. The Finnish Olvi corporation acquired the brewery in 1997.

A. Le Coq Porter continues the company's two-hundred-year tradition as a brewer of porter. It is made from selected dark specialty malts and is dark brown with a dense, foamy head. It has a velvety, toasty, sweet flavour with notes of fruit and coffee.

Colonel Sandels' banqueting table featured plenty of food and drink, according to the Finnish poet Runeberg. Drawing by Albert Edelfelt.

VIII

An officer and a gourmand

Johan August Sandels has gone down in history not just as one of Sweden's last victorious military leaders, but also as a gourmand who appreciated a good spread, including beverages. Sandels applied the maxim 'An army marches on its stomach' (erroneously attributed to both Napoleon and Frederick the Great) in his own way: he never made important decisions when he was hungry or thirsty.

Sandels was born on the 31st of August 1764 in Stockholm. As was typical in university-educated circles in that era, there were many clergymen in Sandels' family. Not because the educated classes were more devout than nowadays, but because there was a long-standing tradition of beginning one's university studies by reading theology. Students could move on to their actual subject of interest only once they had proven themselves in their theological studies. Many were ordained as a subsidiary outcome of their studies. In previous centuries many researchers, inventors and scholars were actually clergymen as their main occupation. The Scotsman Robert Stirling, who gave his name to his invention the Stirling engine, was a minister, as was Anders Chydenius, a major figure in Finnish economic history who also happened to be a staunch advocate of domestic opium production.

In addition to university studies, the cadets' academy formed the foundation for a respectable upper-class career path. Boys began training for a military career in residential academies soon after completing their basic schooling. There they received a wide-ranging general education, including mathematics, geography, French and music as well as military subjects – not forgetting training in manners and etiquette.

Young Sandels arrived at the Stockholm cadets' academy in 1775 at the age of eleven and graduated as an artillery sub-lieutenant several years later. Even in the early stages of his career as an officer Sandels was known as a connoisseur of food, drink and socialising and a man who greatly enjoyed the excitement of gambling. His love of gambling had consequences. In 1785 Cavalry Captain Sandels' balance sheet of debts, winnings and salary was such a tangled mess that he was transferred to the far eastern frontier of the Swedish empire – to Finland.

Soon Sandels and the Finns got accustomed to each other's ways. Two years later Sandels was a major, and in the Russo-Swedish War (1788–90) he commanded a 600-strong dragoon battalion to the delight of everyone, except the enemy. At the end of the war he was appointed lieutenant colonel of the Karelian Dragoons, and in this capacity only the Russians might have been disappointed in him.

Sandels was not a folksy, easily approachable type. Nevertheless, soldiers quickly learned to trust him, as he possessed three qualities that were crucial for a military leader. Firstly, he was always where the action was. Secondly, he was never known to lose his temper on the battlefield, and thirdly, he was unstinting in his gratitude when it was justified. Of course, his troops knew about their commanding officer's inclination towards the good things in life.

But while he – like others later on, including Vasily Chuikov at Stalingrad and Erwin Rommel in Libya – might appear on the front line in the midst of a fierce battle, stepping in for a couple of days' action equipped with not much more than a glass of water and a snowball, he enjoyed a good reputation among military men. In 1799 Sandels was promoted to the rank of colonel and in 1803 he was made commander of the Savo infantry.

Regional defence is not an entirely new invention. In 18th-century Sweden, the answer to the question of regional defence was a system of foot soldiers, called *rotes*. Officers and sub-officers were stationed in official residences in the defended area. Troops for them to lead were conscripted via a land allotment system. The central authority, the Stockholm exchequer, had calculated how much cultivated land, in addition to other tax payments, could pay for the maintenance of soldiers for the empire. Finland farms were small, and there were few houses that were able to maintain a soldier on their own. Sandels' defence area, which basically included the entire Savo region, required an allotment unit comprising four or five houses on average to provide a habitable soldier's farmstead and produce supplies for his use. Periodically – in practice, several Sundays a year – the soldiers of the parish would assemble after church for marching drills, target-shooting and other 'stratagems', as they called them, under the command of a corporal or sergeant. Sometimes the officers would organise larger-scale manoeuvres or drills with an entire company or battalion.

As the Napoleonic Wars raged throughout Europe in the early 19th century, Swedish rote troops were called 'Sunday soldiers'. Sandels was well aware of the serious shortcomings of the system. When officers' pay consisted of the output of their official quarters, many were far more interested in farming than their military role or maintaining their preparedness. Similarly, soldiers on their smallholdings focused on their potato and turnip fields and the casual jobs they were permitted to hold. It was also clear that the landowners did not volunteer their most reliable farmhands, i.e. their best workers, as soldiers. Under the regulations, soldiers had to be above the age of majority and under 40, and they had to meet the army's fitness requirements. The Swedish authorities, with their emphasis on peace, were not terribly strict in their application of these regulations. The poet Runeberg's soldier boy sang of his father who 'took arms at fifteen', and when the army came under threat of Russian attack while on the move in February 1808, the youngest rote soldiers were indeed only just fifteen. At the same time, there were also sixty-year-old grandfathers among the troops, and their ranks also included men with one eye, and those ravaged by disease or hobbling on wooden legs who were forgotten in the army registers, unnoticed and unbothered. But what the troops lacked in battle-readiness they made up for in their knowledge of the local conditions and terrain. This was apparent in Sandels' military leadership as well: he led his troops into battle when and where they were at their strongest.

Though the signs of war were evident, the Russian attack on 21 February 1808 still took the soldiers defending Finland by surprise. They were not equipped for a winter war. The Swedish commanders chose to retreat. The fortresses at Svartholm and Sveaborg (now Suomenlinna, a district of Helsinki) on the southern coast were the only installations that were to be held no matter what. Otherwise their plan was to retreat out of the invaders' path, thereby forcing them to spread out their forces more and more to secure their positions and supply lines. On the Savo front, the command to retreat remained in force almost all the way to Oulu in northern Finland. There in April the Savo infantry was reorganised into the Fifth Brigade, with Johan August Sandels appointed as its commanding officer.

The Fifth Brigade launched a counter-attack in May 1808. During the next five months, Sandels and the Savo infantrymen made their triumphant mark in Swedish military history. Sandels might have been stubborn and arrogant, with a difficult reputation as both a subordinate and a leader, and it certainly is true that he appreciated food and drink a bit more than was necessary. On the other hand, he managed to get the rote soldiers under his command as well as the farmer-officers who led them to perform admirably in battle against the Cossacks and Russian infantry.

The Fifth Brigade achieved its first victory at Pulkkila on the 2nd of May. Supplies seized from the Russians encouraged Sandels to target the real jackpot: a major store of provisions in Kuopio. The colonel was ready to exchange the small personal comforts of camp for meagre rations, lack of sleep and gruelling marching when greater pleasures beckoned. It was a considerable achievement to cover just two hundred kilometres in a week at the time of the spring thaw. On top of this quick march, a 150-man unit led by Captain Carl Wilhelm Malm, a native of Kuopio, seized control of the town in a night-time assault. Sandels' troops commandeered Russian provisions including 1,200 barrels of wheat, a thousand sacks of flour, 8,500 kg of salted meat and 85 tons of horse fodder. There was also beer to wash it all down with. Brewing had been exempted from guild regulations in Finland in 1776, and there were several breweries in Kuopio. There was no shortage of malt beverages in the centre of the municipality they had conquered.

After the conquest, Sandels immediately began moving the food and drink provisions and weapons and ammunition to a more easily defensible site at Toivala on the north shore of Lake Kallavesi. Although the frontline troops of the Fifth Brigade advanced as far as the Joroinen church village over a hundred kilometres to the south in the attack, the Swedes had to begin a managed retreat when reinforcements joined the Russian troops. At the end of June Sandels led all his troops from Kuopio to Toivala. The three-kilometre-wide Kelloselkä strait shielded the brigade from Russian attacks, and they had sufficient supplies for three months. The army did not need to hold their defensive position with empty bellies or dry mouths.

The officer class of the Finnish War on both sides had learned to conduct battle in the Continental manner, like a game of chess: moving ranks of troops over a level field, with the smallest units comprised of battalions of hundreds of men. That sort of war still made sense on the fertile flatlands of central Europe. The reality on the front in Savo, eastern Finland, was very different. Faddey Bulgarin, a Polish-born Russian cavalry officer, described the terrain with horror-tinged awe: 'Finland is comprised of countless lakes and rocks; in some places these are quite high as if piled upon one another, and everywhere they are nearly insurmountable. The small ravines between the rocks have heaps of stones and granite boulders, and they are traversed by fast-flowing streams and even small rivers which connect the lakes to one another. In some ravines grow impenetrable forests.'

It is understandable that the conventional wisdom of frontline attacks and cavalry manoeuvres did not apply in that terrain. Sandels had grown familiar with the conditions in eastern Finland over the years and made excellent use of the 'free warfare' tactics developed at the Haapaniemi cadets' academy. For example, he managed to hinder the Russians' advance with small sharpshooter patrols that shot from the flanks of the troops. Bulgarin cursed the Savo peasants, who he said were 'our most treacherous enemies in this difficult-to-traverse land: We could not diverge from the road a hundred paces without coming under fire, and this . . . prevented us from reaching clear ground.'

An even greater threat to the Russians than isolated sharp-shooters were problems with their supplies. The standard daily rations for soldiers had been decreed in the era of Peter the Great and included food as well as 3.2 litres of beer. In practice, they saw those portions only in their dreams. The Russians were fighting in the midst of hunger, and no beer was forthcoming from St Petersburg. Their plight was not helped by the fact that the Swedish troops managed to seize many of the Russians' con-signments of supplies. The Swedes took as much wheat and liquor as they could, and then dumped the rest in the nearest lake. The Russian troops had to resort to local supplies in order to stay alive. Bulgarin wrote that soldiers obtained bread, milk, dried or salted fish and weak beer from the local area.

Officers on both sides of the front lines observed the same rules of conduct, derived from the customs of the French royal court. The French Revolution and republican ideals had not yet shaken their image of the world. There were strict divisions between the social classes. During Sandels' attack in May–June, the Russian officers on the Savo front missed the trappings commensurate with their rank, so a return to Kuopio was a joy for them. Even though the store of supplies were running low, Sandels' troops did not gobble up all the city's consumables. Bulgarin reported that a merchant lady's house which served as his quarters had plenty of food, which was downed with coffee, wine and punch. Malted beverages do not appear to have been part of the Russian officers' habits.

Things were different a few kilometres away in Toivala. Sandels had some imported drink reserved for the officers' consumption, but he drank the same beer as the conscripts day to day. That was one of his ways of deepening the Savo infantrymen's trust in their commanding officer. Their colonel was made of the same flesh and blood as them – and had the same thirst. As the army's food was heavily salted to preserve it, it was natural that they needed plenty to drink. The crown had decreed the minimum daily ration per man to be one jug (2.6 litres) of beer or malt drink.

So beer was an issue, even though they were in Finland, the land of thousands of lakes. Troops also purchased fermented milk from farms to drink, but the consumption of malt beverages was recommended even for the senior command. A letter from the Swedish War College to Marshal Gustav Horn in 1655 contains the essentials: 'Soldiers must be given sufficient beer to drink or enough money to buy such, so that they would not be forced to drink water in the contrary case and thereby fall prey to disease and feebleness to the detriment of His Royal Majesty and the Crown.' This was also in effect in the Finnish War (1808–09). When hundreds of men spend weeks on end in camp on the shores of a lake, answering the call of nature anywhere at all, the lake water cannot be assumed to be clean. From September 1808 onwards, as the stores of food and beer began to run low and the soldiers' resistance was low as a result of their already poor nutrition, infectious diseases broke out. Dysentery, spread via drinking water polluted with sewage, caused people to get sick and die. In fact, more soldiers died of disease during the Finnish War than of injuries received in battle.

When the army's spearhead division suffered losses in western Finland, Sandels also had to prepare to retreat from Toivala at the end of September. On the 27th of October after the end of a ceasefire, he commanded a few thousand men to defend positions on the Koljonvirta Bridge near Iisalmi, which was under attack by 6,000 Russian men led by General Tuchkov. While Sandels did manage to defeat the Russians who vastly outnumbered them, the victory was not crucial to the outcome of the war. The main army's defeats in northern Finland forced the Savo infantrymen to retreat towards Oulu.

Johan Ludvig Runeberg, the national poet of Finland, composed three poems about the Battle of Koljonvirta, though one of them, *Sven Duve*, is not actually based on real events. Runeberg, who knew Greek and Latin, created a suitable hero for Finns based on the Roman officer Horatius Cocles. It was Horatius Cocles in the ancient Etruscan wars who 'burned bridges behind him' who provided the inspiration for the story of Sven Duve in Runeberg's poem – so the story goes: he set a bridge on fire behind him and defended the end of the burning bridge against a fierce onslaught until all the attacking forces fell with the bridge or leaped into the river below and swam back to their own side.

Another poem is about Sandels himself, and Runeberg undeniably succeeded in embedding Sandels in the Finnish folk memory as a connoisseur of fine food and drink, though he does not mention anything on the officer's table at Partala, near the Koljonvirta river, besides salmon (which was not a luxury at all, because it was available in abundance from the lakes and rivers of eastern Finland), sauce, goose and veal. Drinks mentioned in the poem are madeira, 'Margoo', which apparently refers to Château Margaux red wine from the Bordeaux region, and Dutch gin.

No archival records of the food and drink served during Sandels' time at Partala have survived, but the drinks served to prominent visitors may well have resembled those mentioned in Runeberg's poem. The importance of officers' drinks in managing an army was not underrated. For example, we know that in August 1808 the galeas *Fyra bröder* brought a cargo of port and bordeaux across the Gulf of Bothnia. However, Runeberg's story of Sandels arriving late into battle because of his appetite and the difference in time zones between the Swedish and Russian empires is a complete fabrication. Sandels knew very well what time the Russians' clocks showed and when the ceasefire was due to end. Although the colonel was not seen on the front line at the moment the battle started, that was one of his winning tactics. Sandels launched his counter-attack only when the Russians' vanguard had crossed over the bridge. And he had breakfasted well in advance.

During the retreat following the victory at Koljonvirta, Sandels again displayed his adaptability. When there was no opportunity for a genteel banquet, he would eat and drink whatever his men were having. According to contemporary accounts, Sandels went hungry when the others did and, like other officers, ate porridge made with water for breakfast, lunch and dinner.

Sandels' last appearance in the Finnish War was more festive than those weeks he spent eating porridge. On the 5th of July 1809 he had invited some officers to a formal dinner near Umeå in northern Sweden, to where the remnants of the Swedish army had retreated. Glasses clinked and silver cutlery chinked against porcelain. When a messenger brought news of a Russian attack, the colonel was enraged. His fellow officers said that nothing could be so abhorrent to Sandels as the interruption of a banquet. But the fatherland was calling. The Battle of Hörnefors ended in a defeat for the Swedes, and the leftovers from Sandels' dinner at Hörnefors manor ended up as the Russian officers' breakfast. Perhaps it was this interrupted meal at Hörnefors in Sweden that inspired Runeberg to write his poem about Sandels with the description of a meal at Partala in eastern Finland.

Sandels' successful military career continued after the end of the Finnish War. In 1813 he fought against Napoleon's forces in the Battle of Leipzig, then became the president of the Swedish War College and served as Governor of Norway from 1818 to 1827. Johan August Sandels was promoted to Field Marshal in 1824 – he was the last Swede to be promoted to the rank of Marshal. Sandels, who is considered to be one of the pre-eminent Northern European tacticians, particularly by British military historians, died in 1831 at the age of 67 in Stockholm. Military history buffs and gourmands alike can visit this military commander's memorial at the Klara Church in central Stockholm.

Olvi Sandels

IISALMI, FINLAND

TYPE: lager
ABV: 4.7%
GRAVITY: 10.6°P
BITTERNESS: 15 EBU
COLOUR: 8 EBC

The Olvi brewery was founded in Iisalmi in 1878 with the intention of preventing drunkenness. Master brewer William Gideon Åberg and his wife Onni wanted to offer people milder alternatives to strong spirits. When Olvi was founded, there were 78 breweries operating in Finland. The only one that still remains an independent Finnish brewery is Olvi.

This brewery is located in the central Finnish town of Iisalmi, only a few miles south of the Koljonvirta River, where Colonel Sandels achieved his most famous victory. In 1973 Olvi began manufacturing its Sandels beer, which was marketed with the slogan 'for the finest eating and drinking'. The product range now includes a milder, fully malted beer named after Sven Tuuva, a fictional figure from the Battle of Koljonvirta.

Olvi Sandels is a bottom-fermented, slow-matured lager made of Finnish barley, German bitter hops and Czech aromatic hops. It has a golden yellow colour, a medium-bodied flavour, mild hoppiness and a velvety feel. The labels on the back of the bottles feature little stories about Colonel Sandels' love of good food and drink.

The opening of Germany's first railway line between Nuremberg and Fürth in 1835 was a festive occasion.

IX

Barrels on the rails

Steam-powered vehicles came into use in Britain in the early 19th century. Once Robert Stephenson had solved the teething problems of the railways, mainland Europe also became enthusiastic about railway transport in the 1820s and 1830s. Germany's first railway line linked the cities of Nuremberg and Fürth in 1835. Steam power was harnessed for other national objectives besides passenger transport – particularly moving goods around more swiftly. As the first German railway line was in the southern state of Bavaria, it was only fitting that its first cargo was the national drink – beer.

Nuremberg and Fürth are located in northern Bavaria, less than ten kilometres apart. The two cities have grown together to form a single metropolitan area with a population of around three and a half million, but in the early 1800s they were still independent entities with their own distinct identities and social structures. With some 15,000 residents, Fürth was the more brash of the two: a traditional agricultural centre that was rapidly transforming into an industrial city. Nuremberg, over three times as large, was a city of the educated middle class. In the 16th century it had been a centre of the German Renaissance, one of Europe's leading commercial cities north of the Alps. Nuremberg had lost some of its shine in the

17th and 18th centuries. Voyages of discovery had shifted the centre of international trade to the Atlantic coast, and Nuremberg was not located along any major rivers, which made transport links more difficult. Trade was further hampered by the many customs borders between the many small German states. Against this background it is easy to see why a new form of transport attracted unprecedented attention in Nuremberg in particular. The burghers of the city began considering a railway line between the neighbouring cities in the 1820s, and even the Bavarian royal court became interested.

King Ludwig I of Bavaria (1786–1868) was a progressive monarch who wanted to improve transport links in his landlocked realm. He designed a canal which would pass through Nuremberg and link the Main and Danube rivers. With the rise of steam power, the canal plan was superseded when it became more urgent to put Bavaria on the European railway map. In 1828 the king issued a decree that a railway line should be built between Nuremberg and Fürth. The support provided by the state was mainly in the form of encouragement. Money to build the railway had to be found elsewhere.

Local businesses and private investors were cautiously in favour of the railway project. They were aware that railway pioneers in Britain in the preceding decades had suffered derailments, rail failures and equipment breakdowns. There were risks involved in the project, but the businessmen of Nuremberg had firm faith in steam power. In 1833 they established a railway company that promised an extraordinarily high annual return of over 12 per cent on capital investments. This accelerated the collection of the necessary financing, and the construction of the railway could begin.

The railway was laid out in an almost straight line between Nuremberg and Fürth. The stations were located on the outskirts of the cities so that the total length of the line was six kilometres and 40 metres. A locomotive was commissioned from Robert Stephenson's workshop in Britain. In September 1835 the steam engine components were shipped from Newcastle to Rotterdam, but then came the more challenging phase – the transport difficulties underlined the necessity of railway lines on the Continent. The journey from Rotterdam to Nuremberg of around a thousand kilometres took over a month. The locomotive was transported by riverboat up the Rhine to Cologne and from there on river barges and on mule-drawn wagons to Bavaria. It was finally assembled in Nuremberg, and test runs could begin in late November. Even though the locomotive stayed on the rails, whisking the carriages between the two cities at a dizzying forty kilometres per hour, there were still plenty of doubting Thomases. Newspaper cartoons showed passengers having to push a derailed locomotive back on to the tracks while a team of horses in the background slowly but surely overtook the accident scene.

Nevertheless, as the grand opening of the railway line approached, railway fever had engulfed not just northern Bavaria but all of German-speaking central Europe. Newspapers sent reporters all the way from Berlin and Vienna. The budget for the Nuremberg-Fürth line had been exceeded, which cast dark clouds over the project. On the 6th of December, the day before the grand opening, investors met in the Nuremberg city hall. The budgeted 150,000 guilders had indeed been raised, but the work had cost more than expected. Unless they got an additional 26,000 guilders to pay the debts, the railway's maiden journey could be postponed indefinitely. Georg Zacharias Platner, the director of the railway company, gave a powerful speech in which he reminded the investors of what they had already achieved. They had built a railway line that would be a model for future generations. Everything had been done without public money and – if only the needed guilders could be found – the railway would boost their commercial competitiveness to a whole new level. Platner's speech did the trick, and the investors increased their stake.

Germany's first locomotive, *Der Adler* ('The Eagle'), took wing on Monday the 7th of December 1835. People had come to Nuremberg from far and wide to marvel at the horseless engine. The city's military brass band struck up a festive tune, and spirits were high. When the mayor had finished his speech and everyone had given three cheers for the king of Bavaria, the locomotive could set off. The VIP guests were transported along the Ludwigsbahn railway, named in honour of the king, to Fürth in nine minutes. The return journey departed exactly 21 minutes later, and the next round trip started at the top of the following hour. Then the mechanics escorted the steam engine through its maintenance and into its nightly rest, and a team of horses was harnessed to the front of the train carriages. They did not want to strain the precious locomotive through constant work, so it was agreed that only two round-trip journeys would be powered by steam. The morning and late afternoon and evening trips would run on oats. Horses took around three times as long to cover the six-kilometre journey as the 'Eagle': twenty-five minutes each way.

Journalists spread word of the train's successful first journey throughout the German-speaking countries, stoking interest. The future was steam-powered, people thought, and railways began to be laid in every city of even moderately significant size. The publicity was not the only measure of success. Passenger numbers on the Ludwigsbahn line were better than expected, with over 400,000 journeys per year, and there was no trouble paying the investors their promised 12 per cent return. Shares in the railway trebled in value in the first three months of operation. The first financial year, from December 1835 to December 1836, the profit distributed as dividends amounted to 20 per cent of the share capital. Dividends paid out in the next few years were around 15–17% of profits as well.

Once passenger transport had been speeded up on the rails, the next question was whether goods could also be transported that way. The owners of the railway company had differing views. Some thought it ridiculous that sacks of flour or barrels of beer would need to be moved from one city to another at speeds greater than a horse-drawn cart could manage. Defenders of goods transport also maintained that rail freight would put cart drivers out of work, and loading and unloading would slow down tightly scheduled locomotive traffic. Others looked further into the future. Once Germany's cities were linked by rail, the iron horses would take their cargoes to places where horses could not go. Suspicions about the profitability of the railways slowed down progress but did not halt it. Most people were willing to give goods transport a try.

Bearing in mind how small a change it ultimately was, the first load of rail freight attracted a huge amount of attention around Europe. There were almost as many reporters present as had attended the grand opening of the railway line, when on Saturday the 11th of June 1836 two barrels of beer from the Lederer brewery and a bundle of *Allgemeine Handelszeitung* newspapers were loaded onto the benches on the outside of the first passenger carriage in Nuremberg. Precisely nine minutes after the starting signal, the same barrels of beer were unloaded at the station in Fürth. Germany's first load of steam-driven railway freight had made it safely to its destination. The workers in Fürth got their lunchtime beer a bit fresher than usual, and when the next week's newspapers from the Rhine to the Oder told of the amazing journey of those two barrels of beer, demand for Lederer beer started to extend beyond the brewery's traditional market territories.

The freight charge for a barrel travelling on the outside of the carriage was the same as one ticket for a person sitting in third class: six kreutzers each way. The Lederer brewery had no real need to switch its horse-drawn loads to the railway, but from the point of view of its reputation and the resulting sales, the stunt proved to be a success. They continued transporting a couple of barrels of beer from Nuremberg to Fürth. Gradually more railway lines opened up to goods traffic. It took ten years before freight transport became an integral part of the Ludwigsbahn's operations in 1845.

However small an undertaking it was for a railway worker to heave two barrels of beer onto a railway carriage, it provided a huge boost for the global conquest of beer. As the visionaries of the 1830s had predicted, within a few decades continental Europe developed into one large railway network where goods moved from city to city and even country to country at unprecedented speeds.

There was little need to transport beer in the 19th century when German cities were justifiably proud of their local beers, but not all thirsty people were equally fortunate everywhere. For example, some beer was transported from the Dreher brewery in Vienna to the Paris World Exhibition in 1867. The lager beer spent five days in specially constructed ice-cooled beer cars on its 1,500-kilometre journey halfway across the continent. When it reached its destination, the beer was still frosty and fresh at 4°C, same as when it left the brewery. Over the next century and a half, the numbers of breweries have shrunk and cargoes of beer transported on rails and later on the roads have become commonplace. Anyone can see for themselves how many brands of beer from all over Europe are stocked in their local shop.

The railway between Nuremberg and Fürth did not last as well as the idea of exporting beer to larger markets. As the railway system expanded, the Ludwigsbahn remained separate from the rest of the rail network. In 1844 a new railway station was built in a more favourable location in Nuremberg, and the long-distance trains to Munich and Bamberg stopped there instead. The old station and the line to Fürth remained in use solely for local traffic. Usage dropped, and the last run on the line was made in 1922. The line was later used as a tram line, and nowadays line U1 of the Nuremberg metro runs along that route.

The *Adler* locomotive was retired in 1857. Commemorative postage stamps have been issued to honour Germany's first steam locomotive in anniversary years, such as 1935 and 1985. The railway museum in Nuremberg has a replica model of the Eagle on display right next to its latest ICE high-speed train – with a cargo of two beer barrels.

Lederer Premium Pils

NUREMBERG, GERMANY

TYPE: pilsner
ABV: 5.1%
GRAVITY: 11.6°P
BITTERNESS: 34 EBU
COLOUR: 6 EBC

Professor Friedrich Wanderer, who taught at the Nuremberg Academy of Art, was a regular at the Zum Krokodil tavern in the late 19th century. The name of the pub was the inspiration for the crocodile logo that has served as the trademark of the Lederer brewery since 1890. The history of the brewery itself goes back hundreds of years. It was founded in 1468 under the name *Herrenbrauhaus* and got its present name in 1812 when Christian Lederer purchased it. Nowadays Lederer is part of the Radeberger Gruppe, Germany's largest privately owned brewery group which is owned by the Dr. Oetker food conglomerate.

Lederer Premium Pils is a traditional German pilsner. It is pale yellow in colour and has a mild hoppy scent. There is an aroma of hops behind its typical pilsner bitterness. Some locals reckon the sharpness of the hops was what gave Wanderer his inspiration for the crocodile logo, but there is no known evidence to support this anecdote. The taste of Lederer Premium Pils also has earthy, grassy and slight citrus aromas.

Louis Pasteur in his laboratory in Paris.

Hunting for microbes

Louis Pasteur (1822–1895) is known chiefly for the process which bears his name, in which foodstuffs are heated very briefly to improve their shelf life. Pasteurisation kills most bacteria and other hazardous microbes. Nowadays we associate this process with dairy products, but Pasteur himself was not involved with milk. There were more precious national principles involved behind his vanquishing of bacteria: pasteurisation was meant to unseat Germany as the leading beer-producing country.

Pasteur was a versatile scientist. The origins of his research into microbes had practical purposes: how to prevent wine from spoiling or how to avoid mass deaths of silkworms. In the autumn of 1868 Pasteur suffered a brain haemorrhage, and his recovery was slow. By the time he regained his health in 1871, his homeland was in a dreadful state. The Franco-Prussian War had ended in victory for the Germans. Paris was occupied. Pasteur's laboratory had been forced to shut down. His only son had been stricken with typhoid fever in the army. Following the redrawing of national boundaries, France's best hops plantations in Alsace and Lorraine now belonged to Germany.

Louis Pasteur thirsted for revenge. He wanted to beat the

Germans at their own game: brewing beer. Pasteur's friends said he rarely drank beer, so he was unable to taste the difference between beers produced by different breweries, but that did not dampen his interest. In the 1860s he had conducted experiments on the fermentation processes for wine and beer and learned about the role of heat in destroying micro-organisms. A heating process similar to pasteurisation had already been documented centuries earlier in China and Japan as a procedure to improve the shelf life of alcoholic drinks. Pasteur's experiments raised awareness of the process in the West in the 1860s and 1870s. He was also able to identify the theoretical principles behind the mechanisms active in heating, thus enabling pasteurisation to be utilised on a large scale.

To familiarise himself with brewing practices, Pasteur visited the Kühn brewery in Chamalières in central France in 1871. The brewery was known for its above-average quality and its traditional production methods, but Pasteur was shocked by how long-standing they actually were. The brewery's standard practice was to keep transferring the yeast from an old wort to the new one until the regulars at the local tavern began to complain about the taste of the beer. Then a new batch of yeast would be obtained from a nearby brewery. Pasteur began developing a new production process in which intermediate factors could be reduced to a minimum: beer would be brewed from only the desired ingredients without micro-organisms that caused spoilage. Upon his return to Paris, Pasteur set up a small-scale brewery in his lab and immersed himself in the secrets of beer.

Pasteur achieved results very quickly. He developed a process in which the yeast for lager-style beers was made to grow more quickly and for a significantly lower cost with no need for constant chilling. Thus breweries would not need to resort to cheaper yeasts that they reused; instead each brewery could grow its own yeast, which would reduce impurities in the yeast batches. His central theoretical breakthrough was the realisation that changes in the flavour of beer do not come from spoilage of the yeast itself but from the effects of micro-organisms attached to the yeast. Together with Emile Duclaux, Pasteur improved brewery equipment to reduce the time beer was exposed to impurities in the air as much as possible.

Brewing beer could not be a completely closed chemical process, though. Nor could you kill all the living organisms. The key enzyme in fermentation is diastase, which is sensitive to heat. In making beer, it was crucial to maintain a balance between destroying microbes and nurturing the fermentation process. Pasteur was quite familiar with winemaking from his previous research, but the lessons he had learnt were not directly applicable to brewing beer. The acidity and higher alcohol content of wine made it much easier to store. Once Pasteur had successfully got his brewing and heat treatment up and running in his lab, he wanted to put the process into practice. He did not want to travel to Germany as a matter of principle, and the Kühn brewery in Chamalières was not large enough for his experiments. France did not have sufficient resources for research after the war anyway, so Pasteur headed to England.

The Whitbread brewery in London was one of the largest in Britain. It employed 250 people and produced half a million hecto-litres of beer annually. England was – then as now – an ale-drinking country, so Pasteur expanded his research beyond lagers. He was given a polite reception by the brewery, but as a Frenchman he and his brewing expertise were not taken entirely seriously at first. Pasteur studied the brewery's porter yeast cultures under the microscope – something not previously done in Britain – and soon announced that they 'left a great deal to be desired.' The rather narrow-minded brewery master might have wanted to send the French scientist packing, but Whitbread wanted to hear more of Pasteur's views. His research methods finally gained acceptance when a porter brewed from that batch of yeast turned out to be defective in a taste test. The brewery immediately acquired the most powerful microscope it could get hold of for Pasteur's use, and the fight against microbes began in earnest.

At the Whitbread brewery, Pasteur was able to try out various types of heat treatment. His theoretical scientific knowledge and the practical experience of the brewery staff fed into each other. Pasteur noticed that introducing heat too early made the beer flat. Experiments also showed that too high a temperature prevented further fermentation in the bottle. Through trial and error it was found that heat treatment between 50 and 55°C was optimal for destroying harmful microbes but did not suppress the characteristic quality of the beer.

After returning to Paris, Pasteur continued to work on his heat treatment process in his laboratory. He did not make any significant improvements on his findings from his months in London, though. Pasteur did succeed in developing beers that were more sterile than before, but their taste and smell suffered in the process. Nor did he manage to isolate a completely pure yeast colony. He ordered batches of yeast from different breweries in France and abroad. He added them to a wort and let the beer ferment for a couple of weeks before his final microscopic analysis. There were differences in the purity of the yeasts, but all of them had unwanted micro-organisms in them in any case.

Once again in 1873, Pasteur swapped his lab for a genuine brewery. This time, he worked with the Tourtelin brewery in the town of Tantonville in north-eastern France. He fine-tuned his heat treatment and worked on his microscope research.

In 1876 he presented the theoretical side of brewing beer as well as his practical applications to the general public in a 400-page tome entitled *Études sur la bière* ('Studies on Beer'). It quickly became the brewers' Bible throughout Europe. Both Pasteur and other scientists found opportunities to apply the results of his research beyond brewing. The heat treatment of foodstuffs, which became known as *pasteurisation* after its developer, proved effective as a way to improve the shelf life of dairy products. Many scientists found additional applications for the process.

Pasteur himself realised that some bacteria spoil beer, while others cause inflammation in human tissues. Both kinds could be destroyed with heat. Sterilisation of surgical instruments and medical dressings in boiling water or hot steam, which we now take for granted, was only introduced in the 1870s. Just a decade later, Pasteur's idea had become widespread practice. Pasteur later developed the first vaccines for bacterial diseases on the basis of his research into microbes. An anthrax vaccine was created in 1881, followed by a rabies vaccine in 1885.

As a result of Pasteur's inventions the general quality of French beers improved, but his original goal – of unseating Germany – remained a dream. Thanks to a more sterile fermentation process and pasteurisation, microbes could no longer spoil batches of beer the way they used to, but the technology did not automatically guarantee top-quality beer. A little magic was needed along with the science. Pasteur's colleague and friend Pierre Auguste Bertin once exclaimed in frustration at his endless pontificating about microbes: 'First brew me a decent bock, and then you'll be able to talk some sense about it!'

Pasteur's experiments with beer have brought invaluable benefits for the food industry and medical science. The greatest benefits in the brewing industry were not found in France after all – nor in Germany, it should be said, lest Louis Pasteur turn in his grave. After Whitbread, his findings were adopted most enthusiastically by the Carlsberg brewery in Copenhagen. J. C. and Carl Jacobsen met Pasteur in the early 1870s and set up a laboratory in their brewery to make use of the experimental results from France. The road running across the brewery site was renamed Pasteurs Vej, and a statue of the French scientist was erected alongside it. In view of this honour it seems justified that the Carlsberg laboratory finished the work Pasteur had been unable to bring to fruition. In 1883 Emil Christian Hansen, the head of the lab, succeeded in isolating a lager yeast that was free from microbes.

Whitbread Best Bitter

MAGOR, WALES

TYPE: ale
ABV: 3.3%
Specific data on gravity, bitterness and colour are trade secrets of AB InBev.

When Louis Pasteur came along, Whitbread already had a century's worth of experience brewing beer. The next century was marked by a gradual expansion of the business from a single London brewery to a beer producer known all over Britain. The winds began to change in the 1960s. As a result of corporate acquisitions, the Whitbread Group moved into cafés, restaurants and hotels. Business in these sectors was so good the breweries and pubs were no longer needed. The brewery business, which had been the cornerstone of the company for over two hundred years, was sold in 2001 to the multinational Interbrew corporation, which is now part of Anheuser-Busch InBev, the world's largest brewery group.

Whitbread's London breweries are closed, but beer is still made on a small scale at the AB InBev-owned Magor brewery in Wales. Its Best Bitter is barrel-fermented and is available only on draught. It is copper-brown in colour and has a malty-sweet, bready taste. Its malty bitterness emerges only in the aftertaste.

Carl Jacobsen spent his profits from the Carlsberg brewery on Roman statues and other items for his art collection. Photographed in 1910.

XI

The quarrelsome Medicis of Copenhagen

J. C. Jacobsen lay unconscious in his room at the Hotel Quirinale. The brewery owner had caught a cold while on a family holiday to Rome, his illness had worsened over a period of weeks and on the 30th of April 1887 the doctors gave no hope of a recovery for the 75-year-old millionaire. When his son Carl arrived with his wife from their trip to Greece, the old man awoke and began babbling deliriously. Suddenly the babbling stopped and J. C. formed some comprehensible sentences about the ownership structure of the Carlsberg Foundation, but soon he fell back into unconsciousness. 'Father, are you happy to see me?' Carl asked when J. C. awoke a moment later. 'How can you ask such a thing? Of course I am happy to see you,' his father replied. Those were his final words, according to those present.

Carl's doubt was not unjustified. The relationship between father and son had been difficult. Jacobsen senior had named his brewery, founded in 1847, *Carlsberg* after his then five-year-old son. His father's shadow seemed to follow Carl wherever he went, and he had struggled to come out from under that shadow. As a young man he had tried to marry a girl his father did not approve of. Unsuccessfully. Still in his twenties, he was put in charge of a new division of his father's brewery, but turned out to be too stubborn as an employee. Carl and J. C. were in competition with one another throughout the 1870s. They competed in their production output, the quality of their beer, and finally in their generosity and eminence as art connoisseurs. There was also a six-year period during which not a single word was exchanged between father and son.

J. C. Jacobsen had intended the new division of the Carlsberg brewery, completed in 1871, to focus on top-fermenting beers, i.e. ales and porters. Carl, ever ambitious, could not stomach the idea. He believed he could identify the current trends. Denmark's rapid economic growth and urbanisation caused the demand for beer to explode in the 1870s, but not for ales and porters, rather for lager beer, the Bavarian-style bottom-fermented beer his father's brewery specialised in. Carl wanted in on the same game.

The new division headed by Jacobsen junior rapidly increased its production to the level of the original division under Jacobsen senior's management. J. C. was concerned. He thought Carl was brewing quantities that were too large, at the expense of quality. As J. C. saw it, two very different beers were being marketed under the Carlsberg name, one of which did not make the grade in terms of quality. J. C. considered a long period of cold storage to be a guarantee of quality, but Carl believed that the storage time could be carefully reduced so the size of the cold storage area would no longer be a bottleneck in production. They also differed in their views of whether Carlsberg should be sold primarily in barrels ('same as before', as J. C. wanted) or whether the beer should be supplied in bottles from the plant (as Carl urged).

J. C. Jacobsen was a man of principles. Over the decades he had allocated slices of his accumulated wealth to charity and art. In politics he was a well-known supporter of the National Liberal Party. In brewing J. C. Jacobsen had two chief principles: firstly, that the production process should be based on science, and secondly, that the brewery must not grow unchecked. It should be kept at a size that enabled him to oversee all its operations personally. J. C. also wanted Carl to observe the same brewing guidelines in his own work.

Over the course of the 1870s production from the new division rose to equal that of the main brewery. In 1879 J. C. demanded that Carl limit his output to 40,000 barrels annually and that he stop using the Carlsberg name in marketing his beer. Alternatively, he gave Carl the option of buying out the new division. Jacobsen junior was furious. The two parts of the Carlsberg brewery were now openly in competition with one another, in terms of both production quantities and price.

Although a ceasefire of sorts was achieved when they agreed Carl would build his own brewery and the new division would return to his father's control within two years, their disputes did not end. Carl wanted to call his brewery *Ny Carlsberg* ('New Carlsberg'), but J. C. insisted the Carlsberg name was his property. Finally the ministry decided the name dispute in favour of Carl. Their battle took on some absurd features. The road between the two divisions of the brewery was called Alliance Vej, meaning 'Alliance Road', but as a result of the destruction of their alliance Carl wanted to rename it Pasteurs Vej, after the renowned French chemist. Emil Christian Hansen, a scientist employed in Carlsberg's laboratories, wrote in his diary: 'These two madmen put up ever larger signs in the street, as each of them tries to block the other's preferred street name from view.'

Relations were finally severed in the summer of 1882, when J. C. changed his will to leave his entire fortune to the Carlsberg Foundation. Carl sent two horse-drawn wagons full of items to his father's apartment. The delivery included gifts he had received from his father over the years: books, furniture and works of art. He wanted nothing that would remind him of 'the sort of man who would disinherit his son'. J. C. wrote to a friend: 'A gloomy shadow has been cast over the twilight years of my life.'

Jacobsen *père et fils* were very much alike. They shared the same ambition and obstinacy. Carl possessed a temper that his father did not have, according to their contemporaries. In business, these traits were advantageous – up to a certain point. There was another side to the Jacobsens as well: their interest in social issues and their affinity for beauty. Surprisingly enough, it was their competition in these areas that seemed to hit Jacobsen senior particularly hard.

Rome was both men's great love. In 1862, when Carl was 20 years old, they spent nearly two months in the city and visited countless museums, monuments and private art collections. Though the trip made an impression on Carl, his ambition was directed towards business in the following years. J. C. alone enjoyed the public's admiration as a patron of the arts. In addition to his charitable activities, he supported the beautification of the city of Copenhagen, acquired works by Danish and foreign artists for his collection and paid for the bulk of the reconstruction of the Renaissance fortress at Fredriksborg, which had been destroyed by fire in 1859.

When Carl set up the Albertina Foundation in 1879 to provide statues for public parks, J. C. felt his son was intruding on his own territory. And it was contradictory: even though J. C. did not want his son to become a patron of the arts in his own image, he was even more hurt when Carl did not collect art in the same way he did. Carl preferred French contemporary sculptors, whom J. C. had little time for.

In the trench warfare years of the 1880s, Jacobsen senior was the director of the old Carlsberg brewery, while his son Carl was the head of Ny Carlsberg, opened in 1882. Unlike the cautious J. C., Carl did not spend much time thinking about the companies' balance sheets and liquidity when there was an opportunity to acquire works of art. He was especially partial to sculpture, which he thought was best at reflecting the various subtleties of the human condition. His collection grew haphazardly with works from Denmark and abroad, from classical antiquity as well as the 19th century. His first gallery, built in 1882, soon was filled to capacity, and the same happened with the extension added in 1885. Meanwhile, the Ny Carlsberg brewery was losing money and market share. J. C. shook his head at his son's frenzy as he watched Carl throwing his money away.

In the autumn of 1886 the Jacobsens finally came to an agreement. (The Carlsberg and Ny Carlsberg breweries would be merged a full 20 years later, in 1906.) Once the deal was sealed, father and son planned to return to Rome the following spring with their families. Carl intended to acquire some new artworks in Italy as well as Greece during the trip, while J. C. planned to pay leisurely visits to the Eternal City's countless galleries and gardens. Things turned out differently. The spring rains in Rome gave the elder Jacobsen a chill, which had fatal consequences.

Carl sincerely mourned the loss of his father, despite their years of conflict. His father's shadow did not seem to have lifted completely, though; it was merely evident in a new way. Whereas Carl had previously acquired sculptures on a very broad scale, from 1887 his interest was limited almost exclusively to classical works – the same era and style his late father had been interested in.

Just a few weeks after his father's death, Carl Jacobsen met the German archaeologist Wolfgang Helbig, who would become Jacobsen's art purchaser for a quarter of a century. When Helbig enquired what sort of art Jacobsen was interested in, he replied that his ideal was the Glyptothek collection founded by King Ludwig I in Munich: 'The most beautiful, rich and educational collection of sculpture possible. And because there is not yet anything at all in Copenhagen, we can start wherever we wish.' Helbig understood and set to work. That very same autumn, a collection of eighteen busts of Roman emperors arrived in Copenhagen. More followed:

Greek torsos, Etruscan sarcophagi and more Roman busts. Over the years Helbig acquired 955 classical pieces on behalf of Carl Jacobsen.

Towards the end of the century the Ny Carlsberg Glyptotek gained international recognition. In 1902 Carl Jacobsen donated his art collection to the Ny Carlsberg Foundation, and it found a new home in a museum building completed in 1906. Copenhagen had gained a permanent place on the art map. Carl Jacobsen was said to be 'the new Maecenas', a reference to a supporter of the arts in ancient Rome whose name is still used to refer to generous patrons. With regard to the wide-ranging charitable works and cultural projects of both Jacobsen men, a more apt comparison might be the Medici family, who made Florence into the capital city of art in the 15th century. The same harshness and intensity the Medicis possessed seemed to be present in J. C. and Carl Jacobsen.

There is an interesting side note which links Carl Jacobsen's art collecting activity to the authors' homeland of Finland. From 1887 Jacobsen's art agent Wolfgang Helbig lived in rented quarters in Rome, in a Renaissance-period mansion called Villa Lante. Helbig's son Demetrio purchased the villa in 1909, and from 1946 Göran Stenius, the chargé d'affaires at the Finnish embassy in Vatican City, lived as a tenant on the top floor. The elderly Demetrio Helbig liked Stenius and offered to sell him the villa at a good price. The Finnish government purchased the building in 1950 with funds donated by Finnish businessman Amos Anderson. After substantial renovation work, Villa Lante has served as the home of the Finnish Institute in Rome since 1954.

Carlsberg

COPENHAGEN, DENMARK

TYPE: lager
ABV: 4.5%
GRAVITY: 10.1°P
BITTERNESS: 19 EBU
COLOUR: 7.5 EBC

J. C. Jacobsen's father Chresten had a small brewery, so brewing was in the family's blood. When J. C. learned about lager beers on his travels in Bavaria in 1845–1846, he wanted to try making some in Denmark as well. The first batch was promising, but there was not enough space in the old brewery for the extensive cold storage required for lagers. This inspired Jacobsen to establish a new brewery in 1847, which he called Carlsberg.

In 1883 Emil Christian Hansen, the head of the laboratory, successfully isolated the yeast used in the manufacturing of lager beer. Standardising the yeast (*Saccharomyces carlsbergensis*) prevented undesirable effects from other types of yeast on the brewing process, and its use spread rapidly around the world. Carlsberg was already the market leader in Denmark, and in the 20th century it expanded to become one of the largest brewery groups in the world. Today it has a presence in around 150 countries. For example, the Sinebrychoff brewery in Finland is wholly owned by Carlsberg.

Carlsberg's flagship beer is a golden yellow, light and strongly hopped lager. It has a neutral, slightly malty taste with grassy hops. The Null Lox variety of barley, which was developed by Carlsberg, is used in its production to give it a longer-lasting flavour and head and to improve its shelf life.

When Fridtjof Nansen's ship, the Fram, became icebound on its way to the North Pole, Nansen and Hjalmar Johansen set off on skis.

XII

To the Arctic, powered by beer

Axel Heiberg (1848–1932) was a Norwegian businessman with diverse interests, as well as a politician and diplomat. He gained wide experience of the globe and its natural conditions by serving as Norway's representative abroad, including as the Norwegian consul in China.

Having settled in Norway in 1876 he financed a project of two brothers, Amund and Ellef Ringnes, to set up a brewery. The Ringnes brewery turned out to be a profitable enterprise. Heiberg's enthusiasm for geography infected the Ringnes brothers as well, and from the 1890s onward their brewery provided generous funding for Norwegian scientific expeditions to the Arctic Ocean. Thanks to their support and the success of the expeditions, the brewery owners' names gained a permanent place on the world map.

Fridtjof Nansen (1861–1930) enjoyed skiing and ski-jumping as a boy and was a champion speed-skater. In 1881 he began studying zoology at the Royal Frederick University in Christiania (now Oslo) and spent the following summer doing fieldwork on a seal-hunting ship between Svalbard and Greenland. In addition to his own studies, Nansen was able to practise navigating on the open sea. He also became highly adept at hunting Arctic game. Both of these skills would be crucial on his future Arctic expeditions. He carried on his studies of the central nervous system, birth and development of seals and lower marine creatures, eventually completing his doctoral thesis. As an outdoorsman, though, Nansen did not want to stay cooped up in his study. He longed to be out in the vast expanse of snow, and in 1888 he and his friends skied 500 kilometres across southern Greenland through previously unexplored territory.

That successful journey made Nansen eager for more Arctic expeditions. His goal was now the North Pole itself. Not much was known about the polar regions at that time. A group of islands, named Frans Josef Land, was discovered beyond Svalbard in 1873, but the areas further north were uncharted. Some people believed the North Pole was located on land; others thought it was under the sea.

There were so many icebergs in the far North Atlantic that all their ice could not have originated from seawater and snowfall. The only explanation for that amount of ice could be a Polar glacier that was slowly moving towards the Atlantic, breaking off into ice floes and icebergs. Traces of wood and soil were also occasionally found in the sea ice. Nansen reasoned that the only place they could have originated from was northern Siberia. This theory was also supported by the fact that some items from the shipwrecked sailing vessel *Jeannette* which had sunk near the New Siberian Islands in 1881 were discovered a few years later in the possession of some Inuits in northern Greenland. Thus Nansen made three hypotheses. First, the Arctic Ocean had a current that could carry an iceberg from the sea around eastern Siberia to the sea between Svalbard and Greenland in a couple of years. Second, there was no sizeable landmass to block this current. And third, if a solid, specially designed and constructed ship was allowed to freeze fast to the polar ice in the East Siberian sea, it would most likely drift across the polar region towards the western side of Svalbard, where it would be released into the Atlantic when the ice mass melted and broke up into icebergs and could then sail back home.

Overwintering on a ship in the Arctic ice was not a new concept. Many daring whalers and seal hunters as well as explorers had had to experience it in practice. Many had ended their days there, while some managed to return home. The biggest risks of overwintering were damage to the ship due to the pressure of the ice, and running out of healthy, nutritious provisions for a varied diet.

Napoleon had said that three things were paramount in war: first of all was money, second was money and third was money. Conquering the North Pole did not differ from warfare in this regard. The Norwegian Academy of Sciences funded a good chunk of the project, and in the days when mapping the uncharted parts of the globe was regarded as being in the national interest, a public collection amassed a sizeable sum. A great deal was also paid for by individual patrons – nowadays we would call them sponsors. The largest private donor to Nansen's project was the Ringnes brewery.

There was no suitable ship available, so Colin Archer's shipyard in Larvik was commissioned to design and build a vessel based on Nansen's instructions. Wood was the obvious choice for the hull: a sufficiently tough steel structure built with the technology of that era would have been too heavy. Besides, any damage had to be reparable at sea using simple carpentry skills and tools. In terms of its shape, the ship did not need to be capable of high speeds; above all it had to be stable and sturdy. The bottom of the ship below the water line had to be smooth so it would not be gripped by the pack ice but would rise above it.

The *Fram* (the Norwegian word for 'forward') was launched on the 26th of October 1892. It was 39 metres long, 11 m wide and had a displacement weight of 800 tons. It was rigged as a three-masted schooner, and its 220-horsepower steam engine was capable of a top speed of six knots. As the uncharted Arctic seas might also include shallow waters, the ship's draught when fully laden was less than five metres. Its closely spaced oak ribs were sheathed inside and out with sturdy planking, and the outermost ice sheathing around the waterline was a two-inch-thick layer of extremely hard, resilient greenheart wood. In addition, the entire hull below the water line was covered in copper sheeting, which would be very smooth in ice and also protected against shipworm and other harmful organisms. With a ship like that, Nansen could safely let the Arctic ice carry him towards the North Pole.

Nansen chose Otto Sverdrup to be the captain of the *Fram* and his second-in-command. Sverdrup had been Nansen's companion on the skiing expedition across Greenland. The entire crew for the expedition was made up of 13 men, all of them used to the snow and cold, and many old hands at Arctic seafaring. The ship was equipped to withstand extreme conditions. They took more kerosene and coal than they thought they would need. Their scientific equipment was state-of-the-art, and they had enough spare parts and materials to rebuild the entire ship on a remote island shore if they had to.

The food and drink provisions were in a class of their own. Nansen had great faith in pemmican, which was meat that had been pounded, dried and shredded in the style of the American Indians, mixed with rendered beef fat. This dry mixture of shredded meat and fat would keep for years and it was highly nutritious. The cargo hold also had preserved meat, fish, dried vegetables, a variety of soups, biscuits, rusks, crispbread, bouillion cubes, powdered egg, jams, marmalades, condensed milk, sugar, chocolate, tea, coffee, cocoa and so on. They had everything. And lots of it. Nansen estimated the expedition would last three years, and he calculated a generous safety margin on top.

They took a very moderate amount of drinking water. It was

heavy and took up space, and Nansen knew from experience that potable water was available in the Arctic Ocean, both from rainwater and by melting ice and snow. It was more appropriate to take stronger drink than water. Nansen was not a strict teetotaller, and he certainly appreciated good beer. In extreme conditions like those in the Arctic, however, he considered all alcoholic drink – including beer – dangerous. When consumed in large quantities they produced a deceptive feeling of warmth and security. Even small portions slowed down people's reactions. In a 'living' ice field, the difference between life and death could be decided in the blink of an eye.

The pure alcohol included in the expedition's central store was exclusively for preserving specimens and a fuel for the stoves. As for distillates intended for drinking, a few members of the expedition crew had a bottle or two in their personal belongings. Courtesy of the expedition's patrons, a number of barrels of strong beer brewed especially for the polar expedition were loaded onto the *Fram* for the coming Christmases and other special occasions, and they would withstand temperatures slightly below freezing.

The *Fram* departed from Christiania (now Oslo) on Midsummer Day 1893, left Norwegian waters in July and set a course for Novaya Zemlya and the coast of northern Siberia. As the expedition approached Cape Chelyuskin, the northernmost point in Siberia, they sighted a previously unknown landmass, which they named the Heiberg Islands after one of their financial backers. The voyage continued as the sea began to freeze over with the start of autumn, until the *Fram* became icebound west of the New Siberian Islands at the end of September. By early October the ship was frozen fast and was placed into overwintering mode. They continued to drift northwards, exactly as expected.

The icebound days came and went. The ship's crew monitored their progress by calculating daily reckonings and recording observations of the weather, ice and sea conditions. The shelves in the ship's laboratory filled up with jars containing specimens preserved in alcohol. Excursions brought back fresh fish and roast seal, which Nansen thought was particularly good, once you got used to its strong taste of blubber. They even shot the odd polar bear, whose meat they cooked and ate. Christmas dinner was crowned with the last tankards of Ringnes beer. The year on the calendar changed, but the routine did not.

Months later, in late 1894, it became clear that the *Fram* would not drift as far north as expected, but would be released from the ice west of Svalbard in another year or eighteen months without reaching the North Pole. Nansen, who had not let himself get out of shape, started thinking even more about the possibility of reaching the North Pole. If not by ship, then on skis and with a dog sled. It was a mere 800 kilometres away. On the way back it would of course be impossible to try to locate the *Fram*. Instead, it would be feasible to aim for Svalbard or Frans Josef Land, which he could comfortably reach before the next summer's ice melt, so the total journey would not be much longer than 1,500 km.

At the end of February 1895 the sun began to reappear after the long polar night. The *Fram* was at 84 degrees North latitude and did not seem to be drifting any further north. Nansen handed over command to Sverdrup for the duration of his absence and set off for the North Pole. Nansen had selected Hjalmar Johansen – an excellent skier, expert dog musher, skilled hunter and 1889 gymnastics world champion – to accompany him. They had carefully planned and weighed out 714.47 kg of supplies and equipment, divided among three sledges which were pulled by 28 dogs, all the sled dogs the expedition had brought along save two. They took two kayaks to cross any open water they encountered, and the heaviest things were the men's rations. They took very little dog food along: Nansen, always a careful planner, had calculated that as they progressed the dogs would gradually get worn out, and they could cull the weakest ones and feed them to the rest of the pack.

Already in the first days they realised they would not proceed as fast as they had figured in their test runs near the ship. The polar ice cap is not flat: it is composed of broken and compacted piles and ridges of ice, interspersed with open pits, crevasses and pools of water, even in mid-winter. After a month of running, the first dog was so exhausted it could no longer pull. It had to be put down. Nansen noted in his diary: 'That was the most unpleasant task of the whole journey.' At first the dogs shunned the meat of their teammate, but hunger soon taught them to eat it.

One day the men happened to forget to wind their watches. Johansen's watch had stopped; Nansen's was still going, but it was likely showing the wrong time. That was a severe blow. They calculated their longitude by noting the exact time of local noon in relationship to Greenwich Mean Time or the standard time at another fixed meridian. In the polar region, where the lines of longitude are close together, accuracy is even more important than in more southerly locations. The men quickly wound their watches, attempted to set them as precisely as they could and hoped for the best. It later turned out that their reckonings were off by nearly six degrees of longitude.

As the weeks passed it became clear they would not reach the North Pole. On the 8th of April Nansen and Johansen turned back. The northernmost point they reached was 86° 10' N latitude and approximately 95° E longitude. From there they set off towards Frans Josef Land, which they figured was a little over 400 km away. In fact the distance was nearly 700 km.

Their return journey became a survival tale coloured with hope and despair. The dogs had to be put down and fed to the others increasingly often, and dragging their supplies became more onerous on the men and their remaining dogs. In May they abandoned their third sledge. Their remaining supplies fit onto two sledges, which could be pulled by the ten dogs that were left. One dog after another ended up as food. The last dogs were so hungry their teammate didn't even need to be flayed after it was dispatched with an axe; they devoured it fur and all. Nansen and Johansen made some blood pancakes for themselves from one dog's blood and commented that they didn't taste half bad.

In June the heaps of pack ice changed into ice floes, which moved with what felt like swells of the open sea. Their provisions were starting to get low. Some of the pemmican had got wet and spoiled. Nansen and Johansen patched their kayaks which had got banged up on the sledges and prepared to set sail. They shot a seal on the 22nd of June, which temporarily solved their food shortage. The next day they bagged another seal, and Nansen waxed lyrical in his diary: 'Seal meat tastes good. Its blubber is excellent both raw and cooked. Yesterday we had soup with raw blubber. For lunch I fried some slices which could not have been bettered in the "Grand Hotel", though a good tankard of beer would have been a welcome accompaniment.' He returns to his terse scientific style when he tells how he and Johansen shot three polar bears that had ventured to their camp, lured by the frying fat.

On the 3rd of August the men were once again about to cross a crevasse with all their supplies loaded and tied on the kayaks. Nansen heard a commotion and Johansen asking for a gun behind him. When he turned round to look, he saw a polar bear that had been lurking behind a blind spot come over to Johansen, about to bite his head off. Johansen stated in a calm voice: 'Do shoot fast, sir, before it's too late.' The old Wild West sharpshooters would have lost out to Nansen, so fast did he retrieve his buck-shot-gun from his kayak and fire at the bear from two metres away. Nineteenth-century gentlemen did not lose their cool even in the trickiest situations. Not until the following Christmas would Fridtjof and Hjalmar feel sufficiently well acquainted to address each other by their first names.

Four days later there was open water ahead. The men finished off their last dogs, loaded everything they could into their kayaks and set off across the water. They assumed they were north of Frans Josef Land, but it soon became clear that the land to their left, that is to the east, did not resemble any images recorded earlier. The tide in front of the steep coastal cliffs flowed westwards. Nevertheless, Nansen and Johansen continued onwards, hoping to end up in the southern part of Frans Josef Land, where there would be a chance of encountering other explorers and being rescued, to return to civilisation.

Soon autumn arrived. The nights grew chillier, even in late August, and new ice began to form around the coast. Nansen and Johansen decided there was no sense in continuing their journey. They began to build a winter camp and accumulate food supplies. They used the last few days of the ice-free season to hunt walrus. In the autumn walrus are fat and do not sink when they are dead. One man can haul a walrus to shore with a canoe after shooting it. Heaving a one-ton beast onto the shore is another matter. So the men flayed and cut up their booty in the water on shore, took the meat up to their camp next to the sealskins that were spread out and covered it with another one. The seawater salted the meat, ready for cooking, and nature's outdoor deep freeze took care of the storage. They did need to warm themselves in their shelter from time to time. The alcohol and kerosene had run out ages ago, but they had plenty of walrus fat. Heating and lighting for their shelter was provided by a flame burning on a makeshift gauze wick inserted in some lumps of fat on a metal plate.

The men spent the winter of 1895–96 mostly lazing around underneath their bearskins. It was about as warm inside their shelter as in a modern-day fridge. Nansen thought it often looked quite cosy inside, as the walls of ice sparkled in the flickering light from the fat lamp. Outside it was −40°C, and the wind blew off the Arctic Ocean. Their grease-saturated clothes stuck to their skin and chafed, and they did not provide any insulation, which further reduced the men's desire to venture outside. In February Nansen

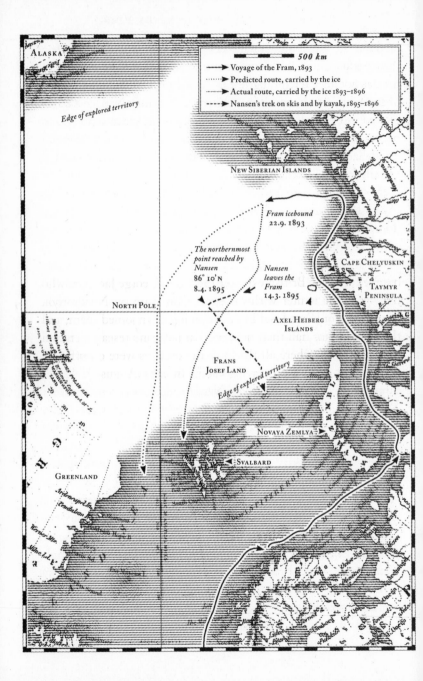

ALASKA

Edge of explored territory

500 km

→ Voyage of the Fram, 1893
⋯→ Predicted route, carried by the ice
⋯→ Actual route, carried by the ice 1893–1896
- -→ Nansen's trek on skis and by kayak, 1895–1896

NEW SIBERIAN ISLANDS

*Fram icebound
22.9. 1893*

*The northernmost
point reached by
Nansen*
86° 10' N
8.4. 1895

*Nansen
leaves the
Fram
14.3. 1895*

CAPE CHELYUSKIN

TAYMYR
PENINSULA

NORTH POLE

AXEL HEIBERG
ISLANDS

FRANS
JOSEF LAND

Edge of explored territory

NOVAYA ZEMLYA

SVALBARD

GREENLAND

noted in his diary: 'Strange to spend the whole winter lying around in an underground shelter without any chores.' He also wrote, 'Our life has not been terribly agreeable,' but then he added that neither of them had lost his positive outlook. The things Nansen said he missed most of all were, in this order: books, clean clothes and proper food, and he surely would not have refused a beer either.

Their journey continued in May 1896. Nansen and Johansen travelled along the unfamiliar coastline, sometimes paddling their canoes, sometimes on land, dragging their equipment in their sledges over the melting snow. The sea ice made banging noises, like faraway gunshots, as it melted. In June they heard a distinct dog's bark along with the banging. Nansen leaped onto his skis, went to investigate the source of the sound and nearly bumped into the British explorer Frederick George Jackson, who had spent the winter with his expedition team on Northbrook Island, part of Frans Josef Land. Soon Johansen joined them, and the Norwegians had their next meal at Jackson's research station on Cape Flora, where all the modern comforts were on offer, as Nansen put it, in a proper log cabin. In early August Jackson's supply ship arrived and took Nansen and Johansen home to Norway. Five days after they returned, the *Fram* also came into port. It had emerged from the ice west of Svalbard after three years of drifting, just as Nansen had predicted.

Later on, Fridtjof Nansen became professor of zoology and Arctic oceanography at the University of Oslo. He served as Norway's ambassador in London from 1906 to 1908 and as the League of Nations' High Commissioner for Refugees in the 1920s. While in this role he devised a document for stateless refugees which came to be known as the Nansen Passport. He was awarded the Nobel Peace Prize in 1922.

The *Fram* continued its voyages in Arctic waters with Otto Sverdrup serving as captain. In 1900–1901 Sverdrup explored Canada's Arctic islands. He mapped the archipelago which is now known as the Sverdrup Islands, located off the west coast of Ellesmere Island. That archipelago belonged to Norway until the 1930s. It was not just the explorers who put their names on the map: the brewers who funded their voyage also had places named after them. The largest island in the Sverdrup archipelago – incidentally the world's largest uninhabited island (43,178 sq km) – was named Axel Heiberg Island. To its south-west are Ellef Ringnes Island (11,295 sq km) and Amund Ringnes Island (5,255 sq km).

In 1910–1912 the *Fram* sailed to Antarctica as Roald Amundsen's support vessel, and it became the first ship to serve in expeditions to both polar regions. Amundsen also commemorated the ship's sponsor by naming an Antarctic valley glacier the Axel Heiberg Glacier. Today the *Fram* is on display in a museum in Oslo.

Ringnes Imperial Polaris

OSLO, NORWAY

TYPE: bock
ABV: 10.0%
GRAVITY: 22°P
BITTERNESS: 46 EBU
COLOUR: 56 EBC

The Ringnes brewery gained a great deal of favourable publicity by supporting Norwegian polar expeditions. It was not fundamentally about achieving publicity, though: Axel Heiberg and the Ringnes brothers were genuinely interested in geographical exploration. The Bokøl double bock which was brewed for Nansen's journeys was part of their collaboration. That strong beer retained its flavour on long sea voyages and withstood the cold better than lighter beers.

The brewery was owned by the Ringnes family until 1978, and since 2004 it has been part of the Carlsberg Group. In 2012 Ringnes brewed a special-edition double bock inspired by the Bokøl which had been made for the explorers just over a century earlier. The new beer, created with the participation of the Brooklyn Brewery's renowned beer master Garrett Oliver, was dubbed Imperial Polaris. Additional special editions were created in 2013 (Superior Polaris) and 2014. Ringnes Imperial Polaris is a dark brown double bock, with scents of honey, toffee and citrus. The taste is chiefly toffee and light hops, which come into their own when the beer is served at a delightful temperature of 10–12°C.

THE ILLUSTRATED LONDON NEWS.

No. 3951   No. CXLVI.   SATURDAY, JANUARY 9, 1915.   SIXPENCE.

On Christmas Day 1914 British and German soldiers in many places agreed an unofficial truce and celebrated Christmas together. Front page from a London newspaper, January 1915.

XIII

Don't shoot! We come bearing beer

In December 1914, when fighting in the First World War had gone on for around five months, a flicker of humanity was glimpsed amidst the insanity of war. Soldiers in many places on the Western Front laid down their weapons over Christmas. Brotherhood between nations was also fostered by activities that brought the young men together, such as football and drinking beer.

At the start of the war, Germany's strategy on the Western Front was to surround the French defence positions and attack overland via Belgium. In the first few weeks, their encircling movements seemed to produce results. Their progress slowed in the autumn of 1914, and in October the front was essentially static. A long phase of trench warfare ensured, with neither side making any significant advance for several years.

The duration of the war seemed to surprise everyone on both sides, from their senior commanders down to the front-line soldiers. Propaganda had assured both sides of a quick victory, but the harsh truth began to become apparent as the autumn rains beat down on the trenches criss-crossing the flatlands of Flanders, dug deep into the clay. Pope Benedict XV had made several appeals for peace that autumn. On 7 December he begged 'that the guns may fall silent at least upon the night the angels sang'. London, Berlin and Paris did not accede to his wishes.

In the trenches at least, minds were open. They did not not know, exactly, to what extent cease-fires were negotiated beforehand. Based on archival sources it seems clear that neither side's high command had any idea what was coming. They only knew of isolated warnings where soldiers were forbidden to plan any mass movements that would endanger or interrupt the campaign. Nor do the soldiers' letters home indicate that a ceasefire was widely discussed. The Pope's plea was publicised widely, and some soldiers happened to learn of it. It is difficult to assess what impact it had, though. At any rate, most of those who participated in the December 1914 ceasefire were Protestants. Catholic units, such as those from France, did not obey the exhortation issued from their supreme religious authority.

The first signs of the Christmas spirit were heard on the 23rd. On the northern fringes of the Western Front, in the Belgian and French border communities, the sounds of Christmas carols emanated from the trenches in several places. Germans might have replied to an English choir, and vice versa. Christmas Eve brought freezing weather, and conditions in the trenches became a bit more bearable when the sludge and mud froze. The singing continued, and people began to prepare for Christmas by obtaining candles and Christmas trees to decorate the trenches.

In many sectors along the front, shooting had been very sparse for the last day. The first peace overtures came on the evening of Christmas Eve. Soldiers who could speak the enemy's language shouted suggestions across No Man's Land. If no one could speak the language, a ceasefire was achieved in the usual way, by waving a white piece of clothing. The first brave souls rose up from the trenches and were joined by some from the other side. In most sectors of the front, peace overtures were initiated only on Christmas Day.

Various views have been put forward on how widespread the ceasefire was. Documents show that around 100,000 soldiers laid down their arms over Christmas. There were over ten million men fighting on the Western Front, so only a small percentage of them joined the ceasefire. Ceasefires took place primarily in the northernmost sector of the front, in French and Belgian Flanders. The Allied soldiers who laid down their weapons were from the British Isles. Most of the German troops who did were from Saxony, as well as regiments from Bavaria and Westphalia.

The Second Regiment of the Royal Welch Fusiliers and the 134th Saxon Infantry Regiment were fighting in Frelinghien to the west of Lille. Later, British Captain C. I. (Clifton Inglis) Stockwell recalled the events of that Christmas Day:

'That night had been very cold. The ground was white from the frost and there was dense fog. We had put up a big sign in our trench that read, "Merry Christmas", and turned it to face the Germans on the opposite side. They had been calling out to us across the lines. Around one in the afternoon the fog lifted and they could finally see the sign. The Saxons started to call out: "Don't shoot! We'll bring you some beer if you come out." Then some of our lads emerged and started waving their hands. The Saxons climbed over the parapet and started rolling a barrel of beer over towards us. A lot more Saxons then appeared without arms, and of course our men emerged too. Even though we had been warned the Germans had orders to attack us, two of our men climbed out of the trench and went to bring the barrel to our side.'

The Germans even had a second barrel of beer. The barrels were placed in No Man's Land and the soldiers from both sides went over to sample their contents. Captain Stockwell realised that as the battalion commander he had to intervene, so he shouted in rudimentary German to the Saxon commanding officer, Captain Maximilian Freiherr von Sinner. The officers negotiated a truce that would last until midnight. Their men were already in a festive mood. They exchanged cigarettes and rations as Christmas presents, in addition to the beer. Stockwell's opposite number from the Saxon regiment did not offer him any beer from the barrel to try, but he understood the hierarchy that was in place in the Kaiser's army. Officers had to be served separately. As Stockwell later recalled: '[The captain] then called out "Waiter", and a German private whipped out six glasses and two bottles of beer, and with much bowing and saluting we solemnly drank it, amid cheers from both sides. We then all formally saluted and returned to our lines.'

Perhaps Captain Freiherr von Sinner's polite gesture was also a bit of conscious reputation management. Frank Richards, who also served with the Welsh battalion, recalled the quality of the Christmas beer his men drank: 'We drank those two barrels dry, even though the French beer tasted like it had gone off.' The barrels were probably from the brewery in Frelinghien, which was not far from the front, on the German side. In defence of French beer it should be said that spoilage is probably not its characteristic taste. If you are dealing with ale that is meant to be drunk fresh, and the barrel has been standing around for several months in wet conditions in the field, it should come as no surprise to find it has gone off.

No more beer is brewed at the Frelinghien brewery. The building was destroyed in early 1915 by British artillery fire.

The bottled beer served by Freiherr von Sinner, on the other hand, could very well have been exported from his homeland. Although transporting bottles of beer to the front lines was not a top priority, logistics archives show that the officer class was given priority access to the fruits of German brewing expertise. Captain Stockwell gave his counterpart an English Christmas delicacy, plum pudding, in exchange for the beer.

Accounts of the later events on that Christmas afternoon in Frelinghien are somewhat conflicting – which might have more to do with faulty memories than the aforementioned barrels of beer. A football match was played in No Man's Land. While some Brits recalled that they played among themselves, it was probably an unofficial international match between Wales and Germany. Some sources mention the final score, too: the Germans won, 3–2.

The current football pitch in Frelinghien is located in the south-western part of town on the Rue d'Armentières, in approximately the same place where it is thought the Christmas 1914 match was played. Football united soldiers in other regiments across the front lines as well. We know that several friendly matches were played on the front in Flanders between the Germans and the British. Based on contemporary accounts, the drinks provided at those other matches appeared to be less elaborate than at Frelinghien.

When the barrels had been drained, the Saxons and the Welsh returned to their own trenches at Frelinghien. It had been finally agreed that the ceasefire would last until the following morning. As the Brits took down their Merry Christmas sign on Boxing Day, a message written on a bedsheet was raised from the German trench. It read: 'Thank you!'

Soldiers' letters home show that the Christmas ceasefire was a significant experience to many of them, which brought a bit of light into their dismal lives on the front. Information about the brief pause in fighting was received positively for the most part on the home front as well. The British papers, including the million-selling *Daily Mirror*, published front-page pictures of British and German troops posing together fraternally. That photograph was far removed from the usual war propaganda hatchet jobs.

The senior commanders did not like the soldiers' unofficial ceasefire. On Boxing Day 1914 British General Horace Smith-Dorrien wrote in his diary: 'This is only illustrative of the apathetic state we are gradually sinking into. It also shows that all of the commands I have issued have been in vain. I have issued a clear order that unofficial armistices, however tempting and amusing they may be, are absolutely prohibited.' Smith-Dorrien was not the only general who demanded disciplinary action be taken against those who had laid down their arms. No court-martials came to trial, however – at least there was that much Christmas cheer among the senior command on both sides.

Not all front-line solders enjoyed the Christmas ceasefire. In the 16th Bavarian Infantry Reserve Regiment, one Private Adolf Hitler fumed to a fellow soldier: 'This sort of thing shouldn't happen in war. Haven't you Germans got any sense of dignity left?'

The Christmas 1914 ceasefire was unique in the First World War. The following year the army high command took measures to prevent anything similar from happening again. The drawn-out war and brutal fighting with gas attacks hardened the men's attitudes both for and against. Brotherhood changed into hatred, and no more toasts were drunk to the enemy's health.

Grain d'Orge Cuvée 1898

LILLE, FRANCE

TYPE: ale
ABV: 8.5%
Specific data on gravity, bitterness and colour are
trade secrets of Grain d'Orge

In November 2008, on the 90th anniversary of the end of the First
World War, delegations from Germany and Wales met in Frelinghien
to commemorate the 1914 Christmas truce. They unveiled a memorial,
and the programme also included a football match. The Saxons won
this friendly match as well, this time with a score of 2–1. After the
match, the Germans brought a barrel of beer onto the pitch in honour
of the tradition. The barrel contained Radeberger Pilsner, which they
had brought from their local area.

After the match played on Christmas Day 1914, however, they
drank local beer rather than pilsner. It was most probably an ale from
the Frelinghien brewery. The region of Flanders, which straddles the
border between France and Belgium, is well-known for its beers.

The *Grain d'Orge* brewery (originally the *Brasserie Vandamme*) is
located in the Ronchin district of Lille, around twenty kilometres
or so from Frelinghien. Its best known beer at home and abroad is
Belzebuth, a fully malted beer with an alcohol content of 13%. The
region's older beer tradition that was already well known by the First
World War is represented by its Grain d'Orge Cuvée 1898. It is an
amber-coloured 'farmhouse ale' (*bière de garde*) matured in cold storage,
with a sweet fruity flavour and mild hoppiness.

Nazi Party leaders drinking beer in the 1920s. As usual, Hitler has a bottle of mineral water in front of him.

XIV

The beer hall agitator

When Adolf Hitler returned from the First World War, he was an unemployed, aimless thirty-year-old without much in the way of education or qualifications. In the war he had made his mark as a battlefield message runner and been promoted to the rank of lance corporal. In August 1918 Hitler was awarded with the Iron Cross, First Class, a rare distinction for soldiers. In October of that year he was seriously gassed in the last major battle at Ypres, which permanently damaged his eyesight and lent a unique timbre to his voice, which would later become famous.

The post-war years were a time of unrest in Germany. Hitler, by then recovered from his injuries, was not demobilized when entering the General Staff of his wartime regiment in Munich. Instead, he was appointed as an intelligence agent of a research commando organised by his regiment to obtain information on a recently failed attempt to install a Soviet government in Munich. Soon after that he was attached to the local General Staff head-quarters as a *Bildungsoffizier*, or political officer. One of his tasks was to keep an eye on propagators of ideologies such as world peace and socialism. These tasks were clearly connected with the Reichswehr, the defence forces of the Weimar Republic carried out in the name of public order and security. Hitler had already decided he would become a politician, and now an excellent opportunity opened up for him to investigate many splinter groups and conspirators.

In the autumn of 1919 Hitler was ordered by the political division of the local General Staff to monitor a small splinter group calling itself the German Workers' Party. One evening he marched into the Sterneckerbräu beer hall where around 25 adherents had gathered. As Hitler himself later wrote in *Mein Kampf*, he was not particularly impressed by what he heard and saw. He had already sized up the 'party' as a bunch of harmless nonentities and was about to leave when one speaker began to present his idea of an independent nation of Bavaria. At that point Hitler stood up and delivered an impassioned argument for a unified, undivided, greater Germany, which resulted in – as Hitler put it – the previous speaker slinking out of the hall like a wet poodle as the others stared in amazement over their beer steins at the unknown speaker. After Hitler had finished his tirade, Anton Drexler, the party's founder, ran after him and handed him a leaflet outlining the party's manifesto and aims. The next day Hitler received a postcard from Drexler, informing him that he had been accepted as a party member.

Hitler's initial reaction was irritation. He did not want to join a party – certainly not one made up of harmless nonentities. He wanted to set up his own. However, he did not refuse membership out of hand. Thus a few days later he duly went along to a meeting of the party's leadership at the Altes Rosenbad beer hall. Four of the top party members in attendance greeted Hitler warmly. Letters from supporters were read out and it was reported that there were seven marks and fifty pfennigs in the party's coffers, for which the treasurer was granted freedom from liability. A contemporary source quotes Hitler as saying: 'Terrible, terrible! It was the activity of a club at its very worst. Should I join that group?'

Just a few days later Adolf Hitler was the seventh member of the leadership committee of the German Workers' Party, which some misinterpret as meaning he was the seventh member of the party. In fact, sources differ on the actual number of members, but there were somewhere between twenty and forty at that time.

The *Bierhalle*, or beer hall, is a genuine German, and more specifically Bavarian, tradition with roots going back to ancient times when the Roman historian Tacitus wrote that the Germanic people enjoyed drinking beer as they discussed important matters. The popularity of beer halls was primarily due to the fact that they did not charge to book a space; all you had to do was buy beer. In German-speaking lands there was generally no need to question this. Beer halls are amenable places for public meetings. Small groups can meet in function rooms at the back, and it is not unusual for an association's office to be located in the back room of its regular beer hall. For those who want to be among a bigger crowd, there is the main hall, equipped with a stage for brass bands or other musical ensembles and usually a podium for speakers. In the setting of these beer halls, a skilled performer can achieve miracles.

Though Hitler, who had come from the cafés of pre-World War I Vienna with their tradition of discussions, was said to have had to get used to the ways of German beer halls, even thinking them sometimes vulgar places, he soon made himself at home in the beer halls of Munich, where he marketed his ideology.

The party membership soon started to grow, going from under 40 in the autumn of 1919 to over 100 by January 1920, and that growth accelerated when Hitler took control of all the party's communications in early 1920. In order to gain more visibility for his publications – and despite the fact that half of the party's leadership told him almost flat-out that he was mad and resigned from the committee – he announced a general meeting would be held in the famous Hofbräuhaus in Munich, which had a capacity of nearly 2,000. Contemporary accounts said emotions were running high at the meeting. As Hitler fulminated, a fair amount of his speech was drowned out, sometimes by supporters, sometimes by a chorus of opponents, waitresses plonking more tankards of beer on tables, chairs scraping and the occasional brawl. Hitler would later write in *Mein Kampf*: 'I knew that now the principles of a movement which could no longer be forgotten were moving out among the German people.'

Hitler diligently made the rounds of the beer halls. Just three and a half years later those unforgettable ideas had found such success that in the autumn of 1923 the Nazis and their sympathisers numbered in the thousands. Hitler had become the sole leader of the Nazi Party in the summer of 1921, and even before that the party's headquarters had relocated from the cramped back room of the Sterneckerbräu into a larger space at the Cornelius.

The shaky Weimar Republic was falling apart at the seams. The *Freikorps*, private armies equipped by right-wing financiers and the Reichswehr in a tacit agreement, were active in various parts of Germany. Left-wing as well as right-wing parties had their own paramilitary wings, and the Nazis' *Sturmabteilung*, or SA, differed only in their superior weaponry and structure of military-style ranks. Attempts at coups and even revolutions were made in the regions and German states. The government in Berlin enlisted the support of the army and the paramilitary groups. A state of emergency was declared in some parts of the Republic.

The state of Bavaria was ruled by a triumvirate of Prime Minister Gustav von Kahr, General Otto von Lossow, who was commander of the troops stationed in Bavaria, and Colonel Hans von Seisser, head of the Bavarian State Police. When the government in Berlin outlawed the Nazis' newspaper, the *Völkischer Beobachter*, in the autumn of 1923 in the interest of public order and safety and ordered the arrest of several paramilitary officers, the Bavarian government announced that it did not intend to comply with that or any other diktats issued from Berlin. Tensions escalated in Munich. Hitler, cherishing his idea of a Greater Germany, now feared something even more than the decrees from the central government in Berlin: he was afraid Kahr's government would declare independence for Bavaria and perhaps even the Wittelsbach dynasty would return to the throne. He decided that the time for great, significant acts had come.

Many litres of beer were downed in Munich beer halls. Old Hammurabi may well have been justified in imposing severe punishments on tavern-keepers who permitted conspirators to meet under their roof.

The Bavarian government announced that Kahr would deliver a speech on the tense political situation in Munich's largest beer hall, the Bürgerbräukeller, on the evening of November 8th, and Lossow and Seisser would also be there. The Bürgerbräukeller was founded in 1885, and when the Bürgerliches Brauhaus brewery merged with the Löwenbräu brewery (the name of which means 'Lion's Brew') in 1920, it also started serving lion-branded beer. In the 1920s the Bürgerbräukeller was also one of the key meeting places for Nazi party activists. For some reason the fact that Joseph Schülein, one of the largest shareholders in Löwenbräu, was a Jew, did not seem to particularly bother the Nazis at the time.

As darkness fell on Thursday evening, the 8th of November, a stream of pedestrians made their way along Rosenheimer Strasse in the Munich district of Haidhausen towards the Bürgerbräukeller. The side streets were nearly as busy. When Kahr began his speech shortly after 8 pm, the 3,000-capacity hall was packed. SA men stationed outside formed a cordon around the beer hall. At 8:45 pm, when Kahr had been speaking for about half an hour, the doors flew open. In marched Adolf Hitler in a dark-coloured suit that was slightly too big for him, his tie askew, and jumped up on a table, fired a shot into the ceiling and demanded silence. The SA men who accompanied him trained their rifles on the audience and positioned a machine gun in the doorway to the hall. Shocked, Kahr broke off his speech. In the silence Hitler jumped down from the table, strode to the podium, shoved Kahr aside, shouted, 'The national revolution has begun!' and prevented the audience leaving the hall. Hitler continued, saying that the national and state governments had fallen, an interim government was being formed and the police and armed forces were on the side of the revolution.

Next to enter was a living legend, General Erich Ludendorff of Germany's wartime Supreme Command, in all the finery of a German general with his gleaming boots and his spiked helmet. Ludendorff, who was favourably inclined towards the Nazis at that point, was 58 years old and suffering from calcification of the cerebral arteries, and he was clearly not entirely certain what sort of occasion Hitler had requested him to grace with his presence. Nevertheless, the audience greeted the arrival of the celebrated war hero with a hearty cheer.

Hitler, eloquently referring to the machine gun, called for calm and silence in the hall and withdrew to a side room to negotiate with Kahr, Lossow and Seisser. Then Hermann Göring stepped up to the podium, reassured the audience and asked them to be patient for a moment: 'We have the friendliest intentions ... and there is no reason for concern: you've got your beer ...' The brass band struck up a jaunty tune and the waitresses brought more beers to the tables.

In the side room, Hitler told the Bavarian triumvirate they were being held hostage and demanded that they support the putsch and perform duties in a new Bavarian government as directed by him. Kahr, Lossow and Seisser – all of whom were descended from noble families with *von* in front of their surnames – looked at Hitler the way only German officers and nobility can look upon a former corporal. They made it clear they had no intention of entering into any sort of collaboration with him. Even the pistol Hitler brandished at them had no effect. This was an annoying setback for the putsch, but Hitler did not let it faze him. He returned to the hall to announce that he had just formed a new government which would be headed by himself. Ludendorff would be the supreme commander of the armed forces. And when Bavaria was purged of its republican corruption, the march would continue up to Berlin, where the cesspit would be transformed into the capital of the reformed nation. The cheer from the audience shook the rafters.

Hitler returned to the side room to speak with Kahr, Lossow and Seisser. They had heard the proceedings in the hall through the door and were now prepared to go in front of the audience and state that they agreed with Hitler's proposals. The atmosphere in the hall turned boisterous. Beer mugs went flying, the brass band played a rousing march and there was some dancing on tables. Only Ludendorff seemed a bit put out that Germany's new dictator was going to be Hitler and not him.

The SA had seized several key buildings around the city, and word reached the Bürgerbräukeller in the midst of all the revolutionary joy that gunfire had been exchanged somewhere with regular army units. Hitler ordered Ludendorff to keep guard over the Bavarian triumvirate and went to investigate the situation.

When Hitler returned to the Bürgerbräukeller, the atmosphere had taken a downturn and people were beginning to disperse. The Bavarian leaders had simply got up and walked out their captivity without anyone attempting to stop them. That same night they issued an announcement that any promises they might have made had been extracted from them with threats and so were null and void. The putsch, which had got off to such a good start, started to fizzle out.

The following morning, the 9th of November, the Nazis set out from the Bürgerbräukeller with 3,000 men marching under swastika flags towards Munich city centre, led by Hitler and his closest Party cronies, with a group of armed SA men behind them.

They passed through a police roadblock on a bridge over the Isar River by force of words and the clout of Ludendorff who was with them, but at the Odeonsplatz in the city centre they came up against a cordon of police armed with rifles. It is not known who fired the first shot. All accounts say that a pistol shot sounded first, followed by a barrage of rifle fire from both directions. Afterwards three policemen and sixteen Nazis lay dead on the ground. During the shooting Hitler threw himself to the ground with such force, he dislocated his shoulder. Ludendorff provided a curious sight. When the gunfire started, instead of hitting the ground like the others he strode onwards, his medals gleaming, through the police ranks until someone managed to stop him after some distance and politely sent him on his way.

At the subsequent trial Hitler was found guilty of treason and sentenced to five years' imprisonment, of which he served only a little more than eight months.

Surprisingly little is known about Hitler's own tastes regarding beer and other food and drink. His friend Ernst Hanfstaengl from his years in Munich said Hitler occasionally drank a tankard of dark beer. At his trial for treason in 1924, however, Hitler claimed to prefer temperance: 'I will take only a swig of water or beer to wet my parched throat.'

All sorts of health guides have always been popular in Germany, and the Nazis' propaganda division always presented Hitler as an aficionado of wholesome vegetarian food and mineral water. The image of Hitler's abstinence created by propaganda minister Joseph Goebbels was not truthful. Every month a consignment of specially brewed dark lager was delivered to the Führer from the Holzkirchner Oberbräu brewery in rural Bavaria. Its alcohol content was less than 2%. The British intelligence service was well aware of this, and one possible method they planned in 1944 as part of Operation Foxley to kill Hitler was poisoning a batch of his beer.

Löwenbräu Original

MUNICH, GERMANY

TYPE: lager
ABV: 5.2%
GRAVITY: 11.7°P
BITTERNESS: 20 EBU
COLOUR: 6.9 EBC

In the 1930s and during the Second World War, the Bürgerbräukeller was a sacred place for the Nazis, where they held elaborate celebrations on anniversaries of the failed Beer Hall Putsch. It was damaged in a bomb attack against Hitler on 8 November 1939. He had made a much shorter speech than expected and had already left the building when a massive bomb exploded just a few metres from the place he had been standing half an hour earlier.

In 1945 the Americans first closed the Bürgerbräukeller and then later used it as a mess hall for its troops stationed in Munich until 1957. It was reopened under the Löwenbräu name in 1958, but it did not regain its former popularity. It stopped serving food in the 1970s and the building was torn down in 1979. Now the site, between the Hilton Hotel and the Gasteig cultural centre, bears a memorial plaque honouring Georg Elser, the man who planted the bomb.

The Löwenbräu brewery's biggest-selling beer is its Original lager, which was also served in the Bürgerbräukeller. It is a pale lager (*Helles* in German) brewed according to the centuries-old Bavarian purity law, or *Reinheitsgebot*. It has a full-bodied mouthfeel. The taste is savoury, slightly malty and hoppy.

German foreign minister Gustav Stresemann (l.) in negotiations with his counterparts Austen Chamberlain (centre) of the UK and Aristide Briand (r.) of France, photographed in Locarno, Switzerland, in 1925.

XV

Lessons in foreign policy from the beer trade

Gustav Stresemann played a key role in forging Germany's new foreign policy after the First World War ended in defeat for them. In the stormy years of the Weimar Republic, Foreign Minister Stresemann was on a tightrope in domestic as well as foreign policy. But he was a skilful man and managed it. He steered Germany with the same steady hand he had used to carry trays of beer in his youth. The nation stayed standing, and its relations with its neighbours did not spill over. Stresemann had also acquired theoretical knowledge of the ways of the world in his doctoral studies. The subject of his PhD thesis was the beer trade in Berlin. Nevertheless, within a few years after Stresemann's untimely death in 1929 the Austrian corporal introduced in the previous chapter, who was less enthusiastic about beer, managed to negate the widespread esteem and respect Stresemann had managed to create for Germany.

Gustav Stresemann was born in 1878 into a lower-middle-class Berlin family. His father was a wholesaler and distributor who bottled *Berliner Weisse* wheat beer he bought in bulk from breweries and sold it on to retail shops. The building in Köpenicker Strasse in the district of Luisenstadt where the Stresemanns lived also housed a bar that was run by the family. They served the same type of beer and small snacks there. A couple of rooms at the back were let as accommodation for travellers. Gustav was the youngest of seven children. As soon as he could see over the bar, he did little chores to help out, but his real interest lay in the economic side of the beer business. Even as a young schoolboy, Gustav knew very well what the price of a litre of beer was when it was in the barrel, and what you could get for it when it was bottled and what sorts of labour costs had to be calculated for bottling, freight and other overheads.

In the second half of the 19th century, one after another Berlin breweries started to acquire their own bottling facilities, which made competition tougher in the market for bottled beer. The Stresemanns were making a living, but Gustav wondered about the future. Carrying on the family business did not seem like a secure option. He seriously considered doing literature and history as his main subject at university, but ultimately went with the safe choice to ensure his daily bread: economics. He enrolled at the Humboldt University in Berlin in 1897, but transferred to Leipzig the following year to study political economic theory. His interest in cash flows in the beer trade had not been extinguished. At Leipzig Stresemann started researching the Berlin bottled beer market for his thesis, a topic in which he had amassed a great deal of experience since childhood.

In his doctoral thesis, *Die Entwicklung des Berliner Flaschenbiergeschäfts* ('The Development of the Bottled Beer Trade in Berlin'), Stresemann presented an overview of the history of the beer trade and analysed the state of the market in Berlin from 1800 to the turn of the 20th century. Naturally he had his own sympathies for the production of traditional *Weisse*, where breweries were in charge of brewing the beer and the wholesalers then distributed it to bars and in bottles to shops. However, he does not express disapproval of the breweries' expansion of their activities to include bottling in his thesis, even though it took work away from many small businesses like his father's. Stresemann believed that economic efficiency was one of the fundamental conditions for success in the marketplace. It was also worth remembering that the breweries and bottlers were not mutual enemies but associates. If a brewery's business was not sustainable, the wholesalers that had dealings with it could not be sure of their future.

Stresemann's recommendations for small businesses were to specialise and work together. It was futile to attempt the transport, bottling, retail distribution and serving with the same efficiency the large breweries could manage. However, you could make a living by focusing on one type of activity. One entrepreneur might handle the transport of barrels of beer in partnership with a brewery. Another might bottle individual batches which the brewery could not handle itself for whatever reason. A third might distribute crates of bottled beer to shops. A fourth could focus solely on operating a pub. Retailers could also safeguard their position by jointly setting up their own brewery.

According to Stresemann's thesis, the enemy of the traditional Berlin stereotype of the unhurried pipe-smoking wheat beer drinker was not the city's beer industry which was revamping its business model. A greater threat to beer drinkers' freedom of choice as well as businessmen's futures was the spread of Bavarian lager beers. It takes time to make *Berliner Weisse*, and production volumes could not be increased to match those of lager-style bottom-fermented beers. Stresemann's main conclusion was that Berlin breweries and beer sellers ought to find new ways of working together and streamline their own operations rather than stick to their traditional roles. That way they could prevent lagers occupying the Berlin beer market the way they had done in Munich.

Stresemann received a good mark for his thesis. Although his research was criticised for being a bit too broad, he received praise for his mastery of his subject. His theoretical view of the importance of the economy as a driving force of history was also lauded. At that point the professors who examined Stresemann's doctoral thesis could hardly know that the insights he had gained from the beer trade would steer Germany's entire foreign policy a quarter of a century later.

After being awarded his doctorate, Stresemann embarked on a career in industrial organisations. He remained in the food and drink industry, moving from researching the beer trade to a management role in the German chocolate producers' trade association. Later he became chairman of the Saxon Manufacturers' Association. Alongside his leadership of that association, Stresemann gradually started advancing in political roles towards the national policymaking level. When Germany became a republic in 1918 after the First World War, he was involved in setting up the liberal centre-right German People's Party (*Deutsche Volkspartei*) and became its first chairman. The party increased in popularity. In 1923 Stresemann was appointed Chancellor and he served as German foreign minister from 1923 to 1929, right up to his death.

Stresemann based his foreign policy on the same principles as those employed in the pub in Köpenicker Strasse or in his analysis of the Berlin beer trade: everything was a matter of balance. In the aftermath of the First World War, a dictatorial unilateral policy based on the use or threat of force could no longer be a viable way for nations to deal with one another. A more lasting solution was to promote cooperation between nations, so a role could be found to benefit everyone. Just as in the Berlin beer market, there was room for large breweries profiting from economies of scale as well as specialised small players, and in Stresemann's view of the new Europe, regional superpowers as well as smaller states could find their own space and strategy for success.

How he was going to sell this pioneering idea to voters on the home front was a different story. When Stresemann was appointed Chancellor in 1923, the German economy was a basket case and hyperinflation had made money virtually worthless. France and Belgium had just occupied the Ruhr region, and there were uprisings in different parts of the country. In October 1923 the Rhineland declared independence and in November the Nazis attempted a coup in Bavaria. Against this background it was not easy to speak in favour of German-French brotherhood or European economic cooperation. And Stresemann didn't even try. He knew that words were what people remembered about foreign policy at home, but deeds were what mattered abroad. It was no use trying to marry the two together. Stresemann spoke about raising Germany's profile, but did not mention to his voters that it takes humility and compromise to do so.

Before concentrating on foreign policy, Stresemann had stabilised Germany's economy and internal ferment. During his term as Chancellor he halted the turbulence of hyperinflation by adopting a new currency, with a trillion old marks worth one new Rentenmark. He understood that a currency has value only if its face value is backed by a tangible equivalent. Even a bartender has to consider who to offer credit to. A captain of industry gets his beer on a tab, unlike an ordinary working fellow off the street. The German central bank did not have gold reserves after it lost the First World War, but the bank undertook to back the Rentenmark with the nation's real estate and industrial properties, which guaranteed its value.

As foreign minister, Stresemann tried to put Germany back on a par with the countries on the winning side in the First World War. He realised that the path to trust between nations began with trust between people. Having observed hundreds of evenings in pubs, he knew what did the trick. State visits were not just protocols and talks. Stresemann liked to sit with his guests in the evening, chatting and sampling the national drinks. This particularly appealed to the French prime minister Aristide Briand. In France, Germany was still considered the arch-enemy in the 1920s, but together Stresemann and Briand managed to persuade the French people that humiliating Germany was not in anyone's interest in the long run. In 1925 the Locarno Treaty negotiated by Stresemann secured Germany's western border, and Germany was allowed to join the League of Nations the following year. Stresemann and Briand, the heroes of detente, were awarded the Nobel Peace Prize in 1926.

Stresemann stressed that he supported cooperation between European nations 'not out of love for Europe, but out of love for Germany'. His overriding view was that cooperation among nations benefits them all. Economic interdependence between neighbours even seemed to be the key to avoiding wars. It took a quarter of a century and another world war before the countries of Europe signed up to the fact Stresemann had declared in the 1920s: 'Look at France today, which has got the largest reserves of iron ore in Europe but also too little coal. At the same time, look at Poland, which has got plenty of coal but an underdeveloped industrial base. . . . The economic merits dictate a union.' In 1951 the European Coal and Steel Community introduced a peaceful economic union in western Europe, which was later expanded into the EEC and then the European Union. When the EU was awarded the Nobel Peace Prize in 2012, the speeches recalled the renewal of relations between Germany and France in the late 1940s and early '50s, but few seemed to know that a similar sort of friendship, cooperation and assistance had been envisaged back in the 1920s.

After suffering from serious heart trouble since 1927, Gustav Stresemann died of a heart attack in October 1929. He is buried in the Luisenstadt cemetery in the Berlin district of Kreuzberg. The German People's Party was strongly identified with its chairman and lost a great deal of its impetus after his death. Extreme fringe parties started to come to the fore, and by 1932 the German National Socialist Workers' Party, led by Adolf Hitler, had become the largest party in Germany. The era of detente and balance was over.

Berliner Kindl Weisse

BERLIN, GERMANY

TYPE: wheat beer
ABV: 3.0%
GRAVITY: 7.5°P
BITTERNESS: 4 EBU
COLOUR: 4–7 EBC

Before Napoleon's French troops departed for Russia in 1809, they discovered wheat beer in Berlin. They termed it 'the champagne of the north'. It would be fair to say the tradition represented by Berliner Kindl Weisse goes back a long way. Similar wheat beer with a sour taste and low alcohol content was known to be produced in the 17th and 18th centuries in various places in northern Germany, but one after another those breweries stopped producing beer due to the global conquest by lagers – except in Berlin. In the golden age for beer in the 19th century, hundreds of Berlin breweries produced Weisse. Its popularity waned in the 20th century, but since the turn of the millennium interest in traditional local beers has revived. *Berliner Weisse* is now a protected geographical designation. Berliner Kindl Weisse from the Kindl-Schultheiss brewery is the only widely known brand, but numerous small breweries also produce Weisse beers.

The colour of unfiltered Berliner Kindl Weisse varies between batches from pale to golden yellow. Its scent is characterised by acidity, wheatiness and citrus. There are citrus and apple notes in the taste. Weisse can be drunk on its own, or the traditional way to balance out its sour taste is by adding raspberry or woodruff (*Waldmeister*) syrup, which turn the beer a red or green colour.

Two cyclists in the Tour de France quench their thirst with beer on the steps outside a rural tavern in the 1920s.

XVI

Le Tour de Bière

'It's better for boys to do sport and drink than merely drink,' Tahko Pihkala, the inventor of *pesäpallo* (the Finnish variant of baseball), reasoned in the early 20th century. His words contained a nugget of truth. Sportsmen throughout the ages have enjoyed a drink. While gymnastics and sports clubs were roped into the temperance movement in early 20th-century northern Europe, sport shares a longer history with drink than with teetotalling. Even the most prestigious cycling race, the Tour de France, has a particularly well-soaked past. There's at least one victory in a stage of the competition that was chalked up to beer.

The roots of modern-day sporting culture can be traced back to 19th-century England, when the leisure-time physical activities of the upper classes as well as the growing working class gradually became codified into sports. And neither class slogged through it all with a dry throat. While gentlemen preferred a cup of tea between innings in their cricket matches, stronger stuff was also consumed after the match. It was also common to head for the 'nineteenth hole' for a drink or two after a round of golf. Participants in the more popular team sports could be found at tournaments on market days in the provinces, where beer, gin and spirits were part of the carnival atmosphere. And we shouldn't forget that beer was traditionally regarded as a key source of nutrition for manual workers. Sportsmen hankered after the same strength London dockworkers got from their porter.

In 1828 the sporting journalist known as John Badcock, whose real identity is lost in the mists of time, advised athletes: 'The athlete's drink is strong ale. With respect to liquors, they must always be taken cold; and home-brewed beer, old but not bottled, is the best. A little red wine, however, may be given to those who are not fond of malt liquor, but never more than half a pint after dinner. The quantity of beer, therefore, should not exceed three pints during the whole day, and it must be taken with breakfast and dinner, no supper being allowed. Water is never given alone, and ardent spirits are strictly prohibited, however diluted.'

Badcock can be regarded as ahead of his time. Distilled alcohol was still a very common sports drink in the 19th century. It was thought to be an overall performance enhancer and to work as temporary stimulant. This practice only started to come in for criticism towards the end of the 19th century. Even then, only the most radical temperance campaigners advocated sportsmen to abstain from alcohol completely. More moderate critics urged them to leave spirits for mealtimes and stick to beer when they were playing. Most did not see any harm in drinking the hard stuff. Cognac was recommended for long-distance runners, while cyclists refreshed themselves with rum and sparkling wine. When Margaret Gast broke the women's endurance world record by covering 2,600 miles in 296 hours (or nearly 13 days) in 1900, she consumed small amounts of beer and brandy during her ride.

One of the best-known examples of the use – or rather, misuse – of alcohol in an endurance sport took place during the marathon at the 1904 St. Louis Olympics. The gold medallist,

Thomas Hicks, started flagging during the run, so the race marshals gave him some brandy laced with strychnine. The first dose did not revive him, so the marshals mixed another cocktail. Hicks perked up and carried on to the finish line. After crossing it, he immediately passed out. He did not suffer any permanent ill effects, but doctors said a third dose of the makeshift performance enhancer would have killed him. Incidentally, strychnine has been used mainly as a rat poison in more recent times.

In the first decades of the 20th century the practice of consuming strong liquor in competition declined significantly. This decline was not solely due to health or sports-related reasons, though. People learned to use other substances to relieve tiredness and pain – including cocaine and heroin.

Beer was still widely consumed during endurance events. The first Tour de France was staged in 1903. There were feeding stations on the stages already in the early years. The stages were long, though, and riders with empty water bottles could be overcome by thirst far from any feeding station. The rules prohibit competitors from giving assistance to one other, so they cannot borrow another rider's water bottle. So the options were to accept drinks from spectators, to take a drink from a spring along the route, or to stop off at a bar. All of these were widely used. Sometimes the whole peloton would agree to pause for a drink. And even when there was no group break, a few minutes' stop at a country tavern for a quick one generally did not have a significant impact on the overall placings. From 1905 to 1912 the Tour was decided on points rather than overall times. When they returned to scoring by time that did not immediately cause more of a rush. In 1914, for example, the difference at the Tour de France finish line between the winner and the tenth-place rider was nearly eight hours overall.

On Wednesday 24 July 1935, the riders in the 29th Tour de France awoke to a cloudless summer morning. The air in south-western France was still, and the temperature quickly rose to over 30°C before noon. The oppressive heat dogged the competitors along the seventeenth stage, a 224-km stretch of flat land from Pau to Bordeaux. The main peloton progressed at a calm speed in a silent line. None of them felt the need to speed up or break away. They had just completed two gruelling uphill stages in the Pyrenees. There were three individual time trials still ahead, and no one wanted to expend excess energy on the country roads of Aquitaine. All indications seemed to point towards a long, uneventful day in the saddle – nothing to tell the grandchildren about.

Suddenly an unexpected sight caused things to perk up. A group of spectators by the side of the road were waving to the riders. They stood behind long tables laden with bottles of cold beer.

Physiological studies on the effects of small amounts of alcohol on performance are somewhat contradictory. A study by Virgile Lecoultre and Yves Schutz in 2009 found that alcohol temporarily reduces power output and therefore overall performance in trained cyclists. Some earlier studies on the deleterious effects of alcohol on performance do not show any clear-cut effect. What is consistent among the results is that when the amounts of alcohol consumed are small, any effects on the work of muscles are also small. The negative effects of alcohol on psychomotor skills such as reaction time, balance and hand-eye coordination are undisputed, however. There are no studies available on the stimulative effect of alcohol or any placebo effect in cycling.

If the scope is widened from just ethanol to include other elements in the drinks containing alcohol, it has actually been shown that beer has positive effects on the performance of endurance athletes. Beer consists of over 90 per cent water, so it can be used as a sports drink if nothing else is available to replenish water, energy and mineral levels in the body.

In the Tour de France, one of the undisputed advantages of beer over water was that the wort was boiled during brewing. Especially when riders accepted drinks from spectators, beer was a safer choice than water because you couldn't be sure how pure the water was or where it came from. If a cyclist drank only small quantities of beer, it functioned as an appropriate refreshment without unwanted side effects.

The beer on offer in the 17th stage of the 1935 Tour de France mentioned above did have one unfortunate side effect, though: it caused a momentary loss of attention. While the rest of the riders gazed at the mirage-like beer oasis, the French rider Julien Moineau slipped unnoticed away from the peloton and powered ahead. At the end of their drink break, the peloton lost some more time on a fracas that erupted when a few riders stashed extra bottles in the pockets of their jerseys. Some bikes tipped over and handlebars got stuck in frames. By the time the other riders got back on the road, Moineau was far out in front, pedalling furiously. He got some drinks from supporters and kept increasing his lead with every kilometre, arriving alone at the finishing line in Bordeaux in a time of 7:34:30. The peloton got there 15 minutes and 33 seconds later. That was the greatest gap in a single stage at the Tour de France since 1929.

Although Julien Moineau never directly admitted it, it is likely he was at least aware that there would be a tempting array of beer along the route. Moineau might even have been in on the plan himself, as many cycling historians assume. In any case, the Frenchman knew to arrange a drinks station for himself for the rest of the race. He had even started the stage with a particularly heavy gear ratio, choosing a 52-toothed front chainring instead of the more common 44 or 50-toothed versions. In the peloton and at low speeds (which he would have expected with the weather conditions), the larger chainring would have consumed extra energy, but it undoubtedly helped when riding alone.

No matter whether Moineau was the instigator of the beer plot, he was able to enjoy the third Tour de France stage victory of his career. After more than 200 km of exertion, Moineau toasted his victory by raising a tankard of beer after the finishing line. One could say it was well deserved. After all, Moineau had missed out on a beer a few hours previously – unlike the other riders.

Kronenbourg 1664

OBERNAI, FRANCE

TYPE: lager
ABV: 4.5%
GRAVITY: 10.4°P
BITTERNESS: 22 EBU
COLOUR: 9 EBC

Aquitaine, the south-western part of France where Julien Moineau rode to victory in his stage, is sparsely populated on the beer map. Most of France's beer industry is located in Alsace in the north-east and in Flanders (*Nord-Pas-de-Calais*) in the north. Cycling and beer are part of the landscape in the city of Strasbourg, located on the German border.

Alsace is a popular place for cycling tours. The Tour de France has often passed through the regional capital of Strasbourg. During Moineau's career as a professional cyclist, it hosted stages in 1927–30 and 1932. In 2006 Strasbourg and its environs were the setting for both the initial time trial and the first stage. The starting point for the second stage was the brewery city of Obernai, 30 kilometres south-west of Strasbourg.

Kronenbourg, France's largest brewery, was founded in 1664 and has its head office in Strasbourg, but production is centred in Obernai. Kronenbourg 1664 is a fresh, malty, fruity lager. Besides malted barley, wheat and glucose syrup are also used in its production. Its forthright hoppiness comes from the Strisselspalt variety of hops, which is prized in Alsace. This beer is the clear market leader in France, with a nearly 40 per cent share of the market.

Members of the Inklings: James Dundas-Grant, Colin Hardie, Robert Havard and C. S. Lewis (l.–r.), photographed near the Thames.

XVII

Oxford's literary pub denizens

Gentlemen's clubs have always been a feature of British culture. Upper-class men typically meet in club premises not open to the general public and spend time on pursuits deemed suitable for men of leisure: chatting languidly, reading newspapers, drinking fine wines and perhaps even playing a game of the sort that requires more mental than physical exertion. Membership in these clubs is restricted, and some clubs do not even welcome guests brought in by their members.

At the opposite end of the spectrum from those premises limited to strictly private use is another British tradition that goes back centuries: public houses, which are meeting places open to the general public – better known as pubs. Anyone at all can visit a pub. The dress and etiquette codes in pubs are less formal than in private clubs.

In the class-based society which Britain most certainly still was in the interwar years, members of the nobility, businessmen, officers and academics were not everyday visitors to pubs. There were some exceptions, however. Since the 17th century the Eagle and Child, a pub in the university area of Oxford, has been a place where students and professors alike could come to nourish body as well as mind. For nearly two decades the regulars at the Eagle and Child included a literary society who spent every Tuesday morning in the same back room discussing literature and everything else besides. Members of this group, who called themselves the Inklings, included J.R.R. Tolkien, author of the *Lord of the Rings* trilogy, and C.S. Lewis, the creator of the *Narnia* tales.

Tolkien and Lewis first met in May 1926, when Tolkien was a 34-year-old professor of Old English and Lewis, aged 27, was a tutor in English philology and literature. Their formal acquaintance developed into friendship over the years, when it emerged that they shared an interest in ancient runes. They would comment on each other's papers and poems, but the real impetus for deeper collaboration came with the arrival of C.S. Lewis' brother Warren in Oxford in 1932. Warren, an open, social fellow, happened to walk into his younger brother's study one Monday morning and engaged C.S. Lewis and Tolkien in a discussion about literature. Warren brought some completely new viewpoints to the conversation, and as their discussion went on, he proposed that they adjourn to the Eastgate pub next door for lunch and a beer.

Their discussion group quickly attracted several new members from Oxford's literary circles, and it started to become influential. On Thursday evenings the members would assemble in C. S. Lewis' rooms in Magdalen College to drink beer and gossip and occasionally dine, as Lewis put it. Tuesday mornings, which often extended well past lunchtime, were dedicated to their meetings at the Eagle and Child, also affectionately known as 'the Bird and Baby'. Like many traditional pubs, it consists of several small rooms with dark wood panelling. Occasionally they took their Tuesday sessions to the King's Arms or the Lamb and Flag instead.

There was no firm agenda for their meetings, and no records were kept of attendees or topics of discussion. However, we can get a good idea of the topics they dealt with at any given time from participants' diaries and letters. Sometimes it feels as if the most important aspect was the socialising. Tolkien described a visit to the pub in October 1944: 'There to my surprise I found Jack [C. S. Lewis] and Warnie [Lewis's brother Warren] already ensconced. (For the present the beer shortage is over, and the inns are almost habitable again.). The conversation was pretty lively.'

The spirit of the gentlemen's clubs was present among the Oxford academics. Although the Inklings' regular meeting place was in a public house, they were a very inward-looking group. Navy officer James Dundas-Grant recalled: 'We sat in a small back room with a fine coal fire in winter. Back and forth the conversation would flow. Latin tags flying around. Homer quoted in original to make a point.' They did not solicit comments from the other pubgoers, and any who wandered into the room by mistake were politely shown the door. If anyone was desperately keen to join, they would not be rejected outright but the core members might give them a frosty reception. Members of the group who brought along guests were not looked upon favourably either. Remarks were directed at J.R.R. Tolkien on several occasions for infractions against the traditions of the Inklings. The only guests who were welcome were those who had been approved in advance by the rest of the group.

The Inklings met weekly from 1933 all the way until the late 1940s. The Lewis brothers, Tolkien and Dr Robert Havard formed the core of the group who were almost always present, but other attendees varied. Over the years nearly twenty different members joined the group, but it was rare for even ten to be present at any one meeting. There were no women members.

At their meetings, members would read their works in progress aloud and comment on them. They discussed literature in general as well as members' own writing. An especially frequent topic appears to have been the relationship between academic and fiction writing – understandable, given the group's close ties to Oxford University. Not all members of the group were writers, but they were all united by their keen interest in literature and mythology. Many were literary or linguistic scholars, but there were also historians, a military man and a medical doctor. The meetings held in Lewis' study stuck more to the subject at hand, whereas the talk was more wide-ranging at the Tuesday pub sessions. The American author Nathan C. Starr recalled his visit while in Oxford: 'I entered, and after ordering my pint of bitter at the bar, I was directed to the parlor, which the proprietor had set aside for the gathering of Lewis and his friends. [...] The conversation at The Bird and Baby was rather casual and general; I do not recall any sustained serious discussion. It was almost entirely informal, friendly talk among men of like vocations and interests.'

The Inklings were particularly interested in storytelling and the imagination. In the 1930s founder members Lewis and Tolkien each drafted a tale set in a fantasy world. Tolkien's debut novel, *The Hobbit*, was published in 1937. *Out of the Silent Planet*, the first instalment of Lewis's 'Space Trilogy' featuring a philologist called Ransom, was published the following year. Draft versions of both these works had been read out to eager listeners around the corner table at the Eagle and Child, just as later manuscripts by both authors would be later on.

The first audiences for Tolkien's *Lord of the Rings* trilogy (written in 1937–49, published 1954–55), C. S. Lewis's breakthrough work *The Screwtape Letters* (1942) and Charles Williams' classic fantasy work *All Hallow's Eve* (1945) were all in the pub. Lewis confirmed in his memoirs that the Inklings' discussions and critiques had a formative influence on his development as a writer. In those years he also cultivated his ideas of a fantasy world that he had harboured since his youth. These ideas took shape in his *Narnia* series, published in 1950–56. Lewis describes Tolkien as being immune to criticism, even though he does mention his distinctly mild-mannered colleague making occasional outbursts in Old English when he got worked up.

But the group's feedback certainly influenced Tolkien as well. For example, after lengthy deliberation he cut the epilogue from the *Lord of the Rings*, even after drafting two versions, because the Inklings did not like either. Tolkien later regretted his decision, and one version of the epilogue was published in *The History of Middle-earth*, a box set edited by his son Christopher.

The Inklings met less frequently towards the end of the 1940s, and it was decided to wind up the group in its established form in October 1949. Various members of the group continued to meet occasionally in the Eagle and Child. In 1962, when the pub was renovated and the 'Rabbit Room' at the back, where they had traditionally met, was knocked through into the pub's main room, the Inklings members looked for new quarters. They did not have to search far and wide. Their new regular haunt became the Lamb and Flag pub, which is directly opposite the Eagle and Child.

Besides the fact that Lewis and Tolkien's books were honed over the years in pubs, beer is also present in their very content. For example, the interior of the Prancing Pony inn in the village of Bree in *The Lord of the Rings* is reminiscent of the pubs of Oxford: 'The company was in the big common-room of the inn. The gathering was large and mixed, as Frodo discovered when his eyes got used to the light. This came chiefly from a blazing log-fire, for the three lamps hanging from the beams were dim, and half veiled in smoke.'

In Tolkien's portrayal of Middle-earth, there are beer drinkers among the humans, hobbits and dwarves as well. Tolkien himself preferred ale, but hobbits also enjoyed porter and mead. Beer also makes an appearance in Bilbo Baggins' 'Merry Inn' song. The description could also apply to the properties of ale:

There is an inn, a merry old inn
beneath an old grey hill,
And there they brew a beer so brown
That the Man in the Moon himself came down
one night to drink his fill.

Gravitas

BRILL, BUCKINGHAMSHIRE, UK

TYPE: ale
ABV: 4.8%
GRAVITY: 12°P
BITTERNESS AND COLOUR: No specific figures given.

There are no commercial breweries operating in Oxford these days, but the Vale Brewery, one of the UK's most award-winning ale breweries, is not far away in the neighbouring county of Buckinghamshire. Vale brews a standard range of eight ales, plus a monthly special beer. CAMRA (the Campaign for Real Ale) awarded the Vale Brewery a bronze medal at its national festival in 2009.

The village of Brill played a special role in J.R.R. Tolkien's life. He would often go rambling in the idyllic windmill-dotted countryside in and around Brill. It also served as the template for the village of Bree in *The Lord of the Rings*. The Vale Brewery has honoured Brill's connection with Tolkien in many of its special beers of the month by naming them after events in *The Hobbit* and *The Lord of the Rings*. One of the special beers was also dedicated to the Inklings literary circle.

The Vale Brewery's best-known beer is Gravitas, a strong pale ale. This golden yellow ale has notes of citrus, resin and hops flavours, with a dry, bitter-sweet finish. Gravitas won a number awards at national and international beer competitions in 2008–2010, and it is also exported outside the UK.

A Spitfire Mod. XXX with beer barrels fastened underneath its wings flying over the Sussex countryside in the summer of 1944.

XVIII

Beer above the Channel

No doubt it's hard work controlling modern-day drone missions on the other side of the world from the central command bunker. Even battle command centre operatives have to be self-starters with quick reflexes prepared to deviate from the rule book. Then again, they don't have to put their lives and health on the line like the fighter pilots of yesteryear. Today their workplaces, housing and opportunities for R&R are in a completely different class. And a pint of local beer at the end of a duty shift doesn't have the same significance to a drone operator that it had for those fighter pilots returning from a sortie back then.

In the days of piston engines and propellers, fighter planes had a short operational range, but on the other hand they could be based at very temporary airfields close to enemy lines. They had to be sent for regular maintenance at well-equipped support facilities far from the front. Fighter pilots in both world wars were famed for the ingenuity they used in finding ways to attach all sorts of other payloads onto those maintenance flights, for the benefit of themselves and their brothers-in-arms.

The First World War flying ace Manfred von Richthofen often used to make detours from his scheduled maintenance and transfer flights to pop home. His Albatros and Fokker planes could take off and land virtually anywhere. In January 1918 Richthofen even dropped a bag of sweets to his 14-year-old brother who was studying at the Prussian military academy.

From the Eastern Front in the Second World War, Helmut Lipfert – who notched up 203 victories and the Knight's Cross of the Iron Cross with Oak Leaves – told how the pilots of Jagdgeschwader 52 would make good use of flights to maintenance units and test flights. In the summer of 1943 Lipfert's squadron was stationed at the Anapa airfield on the Kuban bridgehead to the east of the Crimean peninsula, a typically charming Black Sea coastal area. Cherries, apricots and peaches ripened in the local orchards. The Anapa pilots were welcome visitors at the airfields in more rugged locations, where their chums gladly helped the Anapa pilots to come up with plausible reasons for maintenance, reconnaissance and inspection flights. Things didn't go so well on one occasion, though. Lipfert was forced to do a belly landing in a plane whose payload bay held an ammunition crate filled with just-picked cherries, a present for his friends. Fortunately none of the investigating officers noticed his cargo. Under German military law, punishment for the use of Reich property for private transport would have been swift and severe.

In late summer 1943 a retreat from Kuban began to look increasingly likely, and morale was waning. Because the Messerschmitt Bf 109 was not suitable for night flying, as the evenings drew in the pilots started to grow frustrated, sitting around with nothing to do – and thirsty. Finally one of them managed to arrange a flight for himself and his plane to the large maintenance unit on the rear lines. On his return, as he approached the airfield, a large, strange-shaped bomb was sighted under the plane. It descended very carefully at a gentle angle, and the pilot let it roll to a stop without braking too much, assiduously avoiding any potholes and ensuring no excessive braking would bend the landing gear and cause the load to hit the ground. Underneath the Messerschmitt, replacing the auxiliary fuel tank, was a full barrel of beer – a traditional German *Fass* with a capacity of 157–166 litres – with only a few centimetres of clearance above the ground. While the pilot, Flight Sergeant Heinz Sachsenberg, was not court-martialled for his prank, it was supposedly not repeated. This sort of self-maintenance on the German side of the front was generally forbidden and was more like small-scale smuggling.

The British authorities took a kinder view of pilots' unauthorised actions. When the Battle of Britain began to take a turn towards a defensive victory for the British in late 1940, Winston Churchill made a speech in which he referred to the RAF Fighter Command: 'Never in the field of human conflict was so much owed by so many to so few.' True to their character, the Brits made jokes about this, claiming it referred to the pilots' debts at pubs near the airbases. Yet there was a bitter truth behind the jokes. While many of the downed pilots' tabs did remain unsettled, over months of sustained fighting a few hundred RAF pilots had managed to obliterate the cream of the Luftwaffe, forcing them to indefinitely shelve their plan to invade England. The population of Britain expressed their gratitude in many ways. Many patriotic breweries made deliveries to RAF mess halls, especially those of the fighter squadrons, at a nominal price.

In June 1944 one of the basic prerequisites for the D-Day Normandy landings was the Allies' unconditional air supremacy over the landing site. Although the Luftwaffe was only a shadow of its former self at this stage, the Brits could not dismiss them even as the war was drawing to a close. Despite their defeat on the Eastern Front and the bombings of their homeland, the Germans still had plenty of equipment and firepower. Intelligence reports said they were testing new, phenomenally fast jet-fighters. Many German pilots were skilled battle-hardened veterans who would no doubt exploit every opportunity to strike. Even the slightest risk the Germans might penetrate the air defence to bomb the landing craft or their supply lines was unacceptable. Fast-flying bombers above and ahead of the front line and attack aircraft cleared the way for the ground forces to advance, and the pilots' mission was to enable them to do their job by keeping the skies clear of German aircraft.

With the landings completed, the Allies began to advance deeper into France. To avoid the pilots having to use their flying time getting to and from the front, the RAF had decided to send a few fighter squadrons as far south of the English Channel as possible. In practice this was easily achieved, because there was no shortage of suitable airfields in the area. When they were planning their invasion of Britain only a few years previously, the Germans had kept the airfields in northern France in good condition and even built new ones. Now as the Germans retreated they did not have time to destroy all of them.

The Spitfire – the workhorse of the RAF – had a combat radius of around 750 km (470 miles). In July 1944 just the flight from the airbases in southern England to the front in France and back would have used up half of this. Without advance airbases in Normandy, they would be of only modest use due to the distance to the German side of the front line and back, as well as the amounts of fuel and therefore flying time consumed in air battles. Of course, their operational range could be increased by means of auxiliary fuel tanks attached to the underside of the fuselage or wings. In fact, they created more air resistance and thus actually increased fuel consumption. What's more, the weight of the tanks made the agile Spitfire more difficult to manoeuvre, and every additional litre of high-octane fuel in the external tanks increased the risk of fire. The first thing pilots did on going into battle was always to jettison these auxiliary fuel tanks. A more compelling reason to station pilots at advance airfields was to shorten response times. When the alarm was raised or a mayday call came in from the front, pilots could get there from the Normandy airfields in a third of the time it took to fly from southern England.

It was taxing for the pilots to be in a constant state of alert and readiness, and the condition of the front airbases and temporary quarters left much to be desired. Between missions they soon started longing for beer to supplement the tea and American instant coffee in the mess tents.

In the summer of 1944 a vast flood of supply traffic started coming across the English Channel. All the supplies – even toilet paper – for the D-Day forces had to be delivered to the bridgehead from the operation's departure zone: an amount that was rarely matched later on in peacetime. The decks of cargo ships heading in both directions teemed with troops arriving and returning from battle. Early on, things were not helped by the fact that there were no working harbours. Installing artificial Mulberry harbours helped somewhat. These modular structures made from concrete pontoons and steel piers were built at remote locations along the British coast. They were then towed across the Channel by tugs, then deployed and fixed in place via roadway bridges to the sandy Normandy beaches. Most supplies were delivered straight onto the beach via the landing craft bow ramps. The Normandy airspace was also jam-packed. Urgently required supplies were airdropped to troops that had already landed and later airfreighted in once the airfields had been commandeered. Despite strict schedules and a system of sectors, the rate and volume of traffic was such that the Allies lost far more transport equipment at sea and in the air in collisions and other than from German firepower.

In that rush, the pilots' beer was not the highest priority. When the shipments to Normandy were coming in especially thick and fast, the land, sea and air force transport officers maintained a strict order of priority. Essentials first! Because mild, bitter and pale ale would all have tasted just as good – or even better – to the pilots in Normandy as at home, there was still a demand to organise some shipments.

The main fighter aircraft of the units stationed in Normandy was the Spitfire Mk IX. They could operate from grass airstrips of just 600 metres. Their Rolls-Royce Merlin 61 model, with a 27-litre V-12 engine equipped with a two-stage mechanical supercharger and an efficient intercooler, burned 400 litres of 100/130-octane fuel per hour in cruising flight, produced 1,580 horsepower at 7,000 metres, and had a top speed of 595 km/h. Compared to an early 21st-century car with a 1.4 litre engine that uses 5 litres of 95E petrol to go 100 km and meets the EU noise and emission directives, that could be called almost primitive. The noise and the flames from the exhaust were impressive when the engine accelerated. The Spitfire Mk IX had two 20mm automatic cannon on the wings and two 12.7mm machine guns. And best of all, the Mk IX's wings had fixings to attach lightweight bombs, rockets or auxiliary fuel tanks.

The fighters were regularly brought back from the sparsely equipped airfields in Normandy to the airbases in England for maintenance. The RAF had long had a base at the Biggin Hill Aerodrome in Kent. It was a centre of technical skill and wide-ranging knowledge of aircraft maintenance as well as their design, construction and equipment. And just a few miles away was the Westerham brewery.

Edward Turner, known as Ted, is better known as a designer of the Ariel and Triumph motorcycles, but during the war he fabricated auxiliary fuel tanks for aircraft in his workshop in Peckham, south London. In the summer of 1944, just after the D-Day landings, he got a rather unusual order from the RAF and the Westerham brewery. They wanted him to produce some auxiliary tanks for the Spitfire Mk IX suitable for transporting beer.

In modifying the tanks, he had to pay attention to their pressure proofing and pressure balancing. When the slow cargo planes crowded the lower altitudes on the way to Normandy, pilots would fly above them, often at altitudes above 5,000 metres. As altitude increases, air pressure decreases, and when the outside air pressure is low the carbon dioxide in beer expands, and the beer either foams out of the tank or the pressure inside the tank expands. Turner's workshop solved this problem by constructing the tanks from thicker metal than usual: 16-gauge or 1.65mm aluminium sheet and reinforcing the structure by adding inner baffles. The tanks also had to be easy to drain, also externally. This was achieved by substituting a tap for the standard plug at the base. By July 1944 these tanks were being filled with beer that would soon be flown under the wings of newly serviced planes back to the Normandy airfields. Since there were so many different models and variants of Spitfires in use in the air and intelligence forces, the planes equipped with these new tanks were dubbed Mk XXX.

Another step in the evolution of the Mk XXX happened at the Yapton airbase at Ford in West Sussex. In the summer of 1944 it was a base for repairs and test flights. There was no trouble getting beer to this base, either. In the patriotic D-Day spirit and buoyed by the feeling that the Allies were finally making some real progress after the difficult years of the war, many breweries were willing to supply beer to thirsty pilots for little or nothing.

Henty & Constable of Littlehampton stood out among the small local breweries for its contributions.

Under the direction of the famous Spitfire test pilot Jeffrey Quill, they experimented with fixing a barrel of beer directly to the bomb racks under the wings. They found that two metal rings could easily be attached to the racks which would then accommodate a standard 18-gallon (82-litre) brewery keg splendidly. Calculations showed and test flights proved that there were no problems with weight of the barrels or air resistance, nor with the changes in air pressure in the thick-walled wooden kegs during flight. Another benefit was that there was no need to transfer the beer from one container to another to transport it. And the beer did not pick up a metallic taste, which some purists had complained about with the Peckham metal tanks. So it did not take long for the practice of transporting beer barrels under the wings of planes to become more widespread.

There was one practical problem with having these barrels underneath the wings, however. The ground clearance underneath them was less than the flex of the Spitfire's landing gear. This did not really affect takeoffs from smooth, tarmacked runways in Britain, but landing on the fields of Normandy was another story.

The British pilots' life in the Normandy bridgehead was not all about getting hold of beer. Continuous flying was required to maintain air supremacy, so every German plane thought to be in the area had to be countered immediately with overpowering force. And when there were no signs of the Luftwaffe, the pilots were kept busy providing additional firepower and intelligence to their own ground forces. Planes were damaged by enemy fire, and aggressive flying meant even intact fighters had to be serviced frequently.

On average one 'beer run' a week would arrive at each front-line fighter squadron, and the same flight would also bring and take post and other urgent small cargo items that could fit into the fighter plane. The beer runs became the highlight of the week with typically dry, po-faced British humour. The empty barrels were fastened beneath the Spitfire's wings, the pilot selected for the flight would be reminded of the seriousness and responsibility of his mission, and he would be sent on his way with some good advice. When the pilot returned, his arrival was watched by all the off-duty members of the squadron. Tony Jonsson – incidentally the only Icelandic fighter pilot in the RAF – said few landings anywhere else were observed and appraised as closely as that of a Spitfire returning to Normandy with a full barrel of beer under each wing. A bumpy landing, hitting a pothole or careless braking could cause the landing gear to give enough to make one – or in the worst-case scenario, both – of the barrels hit the ground. With 18 gallons to a barrel and 8 pints to a gallon, that meant a burst barrel spread 144 pints on the runway. Any pilot who let that happen when it was his turn would be reminded of it for the rest of the week – until it was time for the next beer run, and the excitement of watching the landing started all over again.

Clearly, most landings were successful. At any rate, no sources tell of an increase in damage to wings caused by their external cargo hitting the ground, either on take-off or landing, in the summer of 1944.

As summer turned to autumn, when talk changed from the Normandy bridgehead to the Western front, the Allies began supplying beer regularly, so the flights with barrels of beer beneath Spitfire wings became history. While they might not have had a decisive effect on the course of the war or the history of the Second World War, they most certainly did improve pilots' morale on those days in June and July when there was fighting in Normandy in the spirit of Lord Nelson's famous statement: 'England expects that every man will do his duty.'

Strictly speaking, the beer runs were not legal. Customs and Excise tried to tell the RAF they were exporting alcoholic drink without filling out the appropriate customs declaration. However, RAF top brass managed to negotiate a solution.

Spitfire Premium Kentish Ale

FAVERSHAM, KENT, UK

TYPE: ale
ABV: 4.2%
GRAVITY: 9.5°P
BITTERNESS: 36 EBU
The precise colour is a trade secret of
Shepherd Neame.

Pilots in the Second World War enjoyed the products
of many breweries in south-east England. The Henty
& Constable brewery mentioned in this chapter closed
down in 1955, but Westerham is still going. Its British
Bulldog beer is probably most similar to the beers it
produced in the 1930s and during the war.

Shepherd Neame in Kent, founded in 1698, is Britain's oldest con-
tinuously operating brewery. Its cornerstone products are traditional
ales which were also brewed during both world wars. In times of austerity and rationing, beer was brewed with whatever ingredients were
available and sold under the brewery's name without any specific brand.
Shepherd Neame launched its Spitfire ale to mark the 50th anniversary
of the Battle of Britain. It wanted to honour the pilots who defended
Britain from the Nazi threat.

Spitfire is a typical south-east English bitter ale. It is chestnut
brown in colour, with a toffee and hoppy nose. There is a strong taste
of hops, which comes from three local hops varieties: Target, First
Gold and East Kent Goldings.

In post-war Italy, beer became the symbol of the new urban lifestyle. A bar advertising Peroni beer in the spa town of Montecatini Terme in 1956. Photo: Archivio Storico e Museo Birra Peroni, Rome, Italy.

XIX

The American Dream, Italian-style

Chiamami Peroni, sarò la tua birra! 'Call me Peroni – I'll be your beer!' whispered a beautiful blonde in a 1960s TV advert. No Luigi, Giuseppe or Antonio could resist. They left the countryside and moved to the city, prospered and entered the modern era. They thirsted for a blonde Peroni kiss.

Over a twenty-five year period from 1948 to 1973, annual beer production by the Peroni group increased more than tenfold, from 235,000 to 2,564,000 hectolitres. A similar increase was seen in the nation's consumption of beer. Between 1955–1973 the figure went from 3.6 to 16.5 litres annually per capita. The increase in beer-drinking is a reflection of social changes in Italy in the decades following the war, but it is also partly the result of successful marketing. The Peroni blonde was just one example of its numerous ads that marketed the beer with images of a contemporary, affluent lifestyle.

If you watch classic films made in Rome from the 1940s to the 1960s, you can clearly see the changes in the city backdrop – granted, different films depict different districts and social classes of Rome. Vittorio de Sica's *The Bicycle Thief* (*Ladri di Biciclette*, 1948) paints a picture of austerity in the era of reconstruction.

William Wyler's film *Roman Holiday* (1953) shows the optimism of the economic upturn in the 1950s. Federico Fellini's cityscape screams 'now', with endless little Fiats and garish adverts in his anthology film *Boccaccio '70* (the episode *Le tentazioni del dottor Antonio*, 1962).

Italy lay in ruins after the Second World War. It had lost all its colonies, and reconstruction had to start from scratch. Its diverse agriculture created the foundations to get by and get on, but it could not provide employment for the growing population in the longer term. Migration from rural areas increased, providing an ample cheap workforce for industries that were getting back on their feet. Beginning in the late 1940s, Italy was one of the fastest-growing economies in post-war Europe.

Italians' image of America had traditionally been positive. Between 1900 and 1914 nearly three million Italians emigrated across the Atlantic. Although life in their new homeland was not as cushy as they had imagined for those who were unskilled and could not speak English, they did not moan about it in their letters to the old country. They were there to achieve the American Dream, and many Italian-Americans did just that – one way or another. The mob boss Al Capone and opera tenor Enrico Caruso were famous all over the world. The reign of the Fascists and being on opposite sides in the Second World War briefly dimmed America's appeal in Italian minds, but the foundations for post-war friendship were there.

Mussolini's reputation crumbled during the course of the war and American soldiers were welcomed as liberators in 1943–44. Of course, there were dissenters as well, but they knew to keep quiet. As in other parts of Europe, the soldiers handed out chewing gum, chocolate and other items that felt like unimaginable luxuries in a country living under wartime privation. In America you had to be rich! A more tangible sign of the wealth on the other side of the Atlantic was the aid the US gave European countries under the Marshall Plan in 1948–1951. Italy was given $1.2 billion for reconstruction. Only Britain, France and Germany received more.

Not everyone wanted to emigrate, though. There was work to be had in Italy after the war, too. The economy in the northern cities picked up. While many were still leaving for places abroad including South America, opinions began to change. You didn't have to cross the ocean to chase the dream – it could come true in Italy. Urbanisation meant a change in lifestyles, which gave Italy's beer industry an opportunity to secure a bigger chunk of the drinks market.

Beer consumption was still low in Italy at the end of the 1940s. In the southern and central parts of the country, beer was drunk mainly as a thirst quencher in the summer. People drank water or wine with meals. When people from villages in the south arrived in northern industrial cities in search of work, they found a very different food culture. People preferred rice and polenta to pasta. Frying was done in butter, not olive oil. Wine was very popular in the north as well, but in areas that had been under Austrian rule in the 19th century people often drank beer.

Northern breweries such as Moretti in areas that attracted new residents achieved record sales year after year. Peroni, based in Rome, had to rise to the challenge. It acquired some small northern breweries, but its key insight was that there was the most room on the market in places where people did not traditionally drink beer. Geography became Peroni's strong point. It went after growth in southern and central Italy. But in order to achieve it, they would have to change people's attitudes.

In the 1950s Italy experienced an economic miracle, the *miracolo economico*. Consumer demand increased dramatically. The new Italians wanted to live a modern urban lifestyle, which entailed consumption. Peroni had updated its brewing facilities in the early

1950s with American equipment. The company's management also went on a fact-finding trip to learn about the American marketing system and realised the importance of having a strong brand name in a changing society. Consumers wanted to make choices and express their freedom by buying exactly the brand of bicycle, cigarettes or beer they wanted.

Peroni made itself visible. The company wanted a loyal customer base that would order Peroni by name and not just any *birra*. They built the brand by giving promotional items to bars and cafés: ashtrays, tables, chairs and awnings. A particularly popular item was a giant bottle cap that said *Birra Peroni*. The bottle cap – itself an American invention – was a very recent arrival in 1950s Italy, and Peroni used it to create an image of high quality.

Italians' thirst for beer was stimulated in the 1950s with an advertising campaign that started off quite edifying. Beer was said to be 'exceptionally suitable for the elderly, women and youths' and people were urged to drink it 'in all seasons, particularly during the hot summer months'. They were also reminded: 'Don't leave beer off your daily shopping list.' Big-name stars were chosen to represent the brand, including Anita Ekberg, who had achieved icon status in the film *La Dolce Vita* (1960). Beer was associated with images of modernity, urbanness and even success.

The ads worked. Sales of Peroni doubled between 1958 and 1963. There was a market for other breweries' products as well – sometimes so much so that production could not keep up with demand. Meanwhile wine consumption decreased. Part of the reason might have been the increase in beer drinking, but the general increase in affluence and urbanisation also contributed to the change. Instead of a factory worker drinking wine from the vineyards of his home village, it was easy for him to have an *aperitivo* in a bar and sit and watch television for a bit. Or he might have a beer while munching on antipasti. Regular television broadcasts had started in Italy in 1954, instantly resulting in an increase in the popularity of bars. People came to the bar to watch TV programmes. Television sets would not become common items in Italian homes until the following decade.

By the early 1960s Peroni had already achieved a solid place in the national beer market. It was the market leader, with around a third of total sales. The next chapter in its success story was written in 1964 when it launched a premium lager, Nastro Azzurro. The name, which means 'blue ribbon', referred to the general atmosphere of the 1960s. It was nostalgic as well as dynamic and forward-looking. In the early 20th century a blue ribbon was an unofficial award given to the ocean liner that achieved the greatest average speed on an Atlantic crossing. The symbol became widely known in 1910, when the *RMS Mauretania*'s record speed was 26 knots (48 km/h).

The Nastro Azzurro brand promoted images of Americanness and modernity. Its name was a direct reference to turn-of-the-century emigration across the Atlantic, as its streamlined label with a white background gave an impression of modernity. It stood out from the other Italian brands of the day. Another innovation was that Nastro Azzurro was sold in cans, which had not been very popular in Italy before. Its popularity grew even more when the Peroni blonde, a pretty young woman named Solvi Stübing, appeared in print and TV adverts in a skimpy sailor outfit. She was replaced by new blonde beauties in the 1970s. Adverts starring the Peroni blondes continued for decades, with one in 2006 clearly referencing Fellini's *La Dolce Vita*.

The success of Peroni and other Italian breweries continued just as long as their economic miracle. When the 1973 oil crisis plunged Italy into recession, demand for beer also fell. A return to *mamma*'s cooking and grandpa's wines seemed like a sensible move for impoverished Pierluigi. But when the nation's economy and urbanisation resumed their growth in the late 1970s, demand for beer returned as well. Italians' annual beer consumption increased in the 1980s and '90s and levelled out in the 2000s at around 30 litres per capita.

Peroni Nastro Azzurro

ROME, ITALY

TYPE: lager
ABV: 5.1%
GRAVITY: 11.4°P
BITTERNESS: 18.4 EBU
COLOUR: 5.8 EBC

Francesco Peroni founded the brewery that bears his name in the northern Italian town of Vigevano in 1846. Attracted by the opportunities for growth in Rome, he relocated his brewery operations to the capital of the newly united Italy in the 1860s and 1870s. In the early 20th century, the family-run business expanded into all of southern Italy. Beer really started to flow into the international market from the 1960s onwards. In 2003 Peroni was acquired but the multinational SABMiller corporation.

Peroni Nastro Azzurro is a pale, medium-bodied lager. Nastro Azzurro was launched in 1964 and the following year it was awarded a gold medal in Perugia as the world's best lager. As is typical with Italian lagers, its maltiness is lightened with corn. It has a fresh taste with notes of grain and a slightly bitter finish from the hops.

Czech President Václav Havel (l.) often served beer to his official guests.
His companions at his table at U Zlatého Tygra *in 1994 were*
US President Bill Clinton and UN Ambassador Madeleine Albright.
Photo: Ondřej Němec.

XX

From the brewery to the presidency

The Czech screenwriter Václav Havel (1936–2011) played a key role in the fall of the Communist regime in Eastern Europe. The hero of the 1989 Velvet Revolution became the last president of Czechoslovakia and then the first president of the Czech Republic. But Havel's CV was not limited to just the theatre and politics. He also spent a little under a year working in a brewery.

Prior to the Communists' rise to power in 1948, Havel's father was a successful businessman. The taint of that bourgeois legacy caused the authorities to view young Václav with suspicion at first. He was refused admission to university to study humanities in 1955. The two years Havel spent in the Czech Technical University did not change the young man's mind or make an engineer out of him. He was drawn to the theatre. In the 1960s he gained an international reputation for his absurdist plays that portrayed the senselessness of bureaucracy.

After the Soviet occupation of 1968, Havel's plays were banned from being performed in Czechoslovakia. But he was not left empty-handed. His family had a city apartment in Prague, and Havel had purchased a peasant cottage in Hrádeček, near the city of Trutnov in the northern part of the country, the previous year.

The events of 1968 had meant unprecedented success for Havel's plays in the West. The royalties guaranteed him a steady cash flow.

As the relevance of his plays waned and his income declined, Havel started to run short of funds. He was still writing a great deal, but his political essays were only distributed in underground publications in Czechoslovakia. He started to become frustrated by this inactivity. In Prague his every movement was monitored, so Havel and his wife Olga spent more time at their rural home in Hrádeček. Looking back on the early 1970s, Havel described them as a period of 'semi-voluntary internal exile'.

In the winter of 1974 Havel was looking for a job, spurred by his concern about being idle and a need to have something stimulating to do. He was not in any immediate danger of going bankrupt.

The Trutnov brewery was located around ten kilometres from Hrádeček. At his job interview Havel admitted to the brewmaster that he was a dissident, but it didn't matter. 'Oh, we've got gypsies working here as well,' the brewmaster replied. He hired Havel for the warehouse. Two days later the local Communist Party bigwigs got wind of it and decreed that the brewery could not hire the politically suspect Havel. The damage had already been done, however, and his employment contract was signed. The Party did its duty: agents of the secret police bugged the brewery premises and instructed some workers known to be loyal communists to keep an eye on the new arrival.

Havel got what he had come to the brewery for: things to do. The slightly-built man's thoughts were successfully kept away from the world of poetry, plays and politics as he lugged sacks of hops and barley and shifted barrels in the chilly warehouse. A hundred-litre barrel weighs 95 kilograms when empty and over double that when full. Jan Špalek, Havel's supervisor in those days, recalled: 'It was tough for him at first. The poor guy was freezing all the time.' Gradually he built up his strength, and the barrels started to roll more easily. Spring arrived. To the disappointment of the secret police, Havel did not talk politics at work. His colleagues remembered him as 'the silent type', 'a good mate', 'hard-working' and 'a guy who was just like us'.

The playwright never fully lost his subtly provocative nature. Every morning he would drive to work in his Mercedes, purchased with Western hard currency. Very early on Havel was instructed that he could not drive it and park on the brewery premises. He was astonished by the ban, but his colleagues pointed out the surrounding reality: 'The brewery director drives a small Moskvitš, the brewmaster drives a Moskvitš ... And you drive your arse around in a Mercedes.' From that point on, Havel parked his car in front of the brewery, until that was banned as well as an 'annoyance to the proletariat'. The next morning the dutiful brewery worker drove up and parked outside the Communist Party offices. The workers did not seem to take offence at that.

A few months later Havel got a promotion from the warehouse to the brewery proper, in the filtration room. Decades later, he ironically recalled his job as being 'spoiling the beer'. There was an explanation: 'Beer tastes best right after brewing, because it still contains a bit of live yeast which lends it some aromas. But you cannot leave beer like that, because the barrels might explode, so it has to be filtered before it is taken out. This makes the flavour worse.'

Havel left his job in November 1974. The reason was simply that he could no longer get to the brewery the same way as before. When winter came, the secret police decreed that the local road that went past Havel's house would not be ploughed. Havel did not switch to walking; instead, he quit. The brewery job had not paid as much as Havel had hoped. A third of his monthly pay packet of 2,000 korunas went on petrol for his Mercedes. Nevertheless, the nine months he had spent at the brewery were rewarding as an experience, and in a certain sense even epoch-making in terms of his entire career.

In early 1975 Havel wrote a one-act play entitled *Audience*. He recalled that the play took shape quickly, over one or two nights. The characters are Ferdinand Vaněk – Havel's alter ego, an intellectual who goes to work in a brewery – and his supervisor, who is rather partial to beer. The supervisor receives a communique ordering him to report on Vaněk's activities to the authorities. The problem is, the supervisor is not good with words, so he asks Vaněk to observe himself and write up reports in the supervisor's name.

The play was distributed via underground channels and even made it into the hands of workers at the Trutnov brewery. No one failed to notice who the real-life figures behind Vaněk and his supervisor were. The brewmaster Vilém Kasper was known as a friendly but boozy unfortunate. Vaněk became a recurring character in two more plays: *Unveiling* (*Vernisáž*, 1975) and *Protest*, 1978.

After *Audience*, Havel was re-energised. In April 1975 he wrote an open letter to General Secretary Gustáv Husák of the Czechoslovak Communist Party. That sealed Havel's fate. He was now an outcast in the eyes of the regime – as well as a leading dissident. He solidified his position as a critic of the Communist regime two years later, when he was one of the first signatories to the Charter 77 manifesto.

Many other Czechoslovak dissidents ended up doing menial work in the 1970s when the Party banned them from jobs commensurate with their education. For example, the journalist Jiří Dienstbier spent some time working as a furnace stoker and night watchman at the Staropramen brewery in Prague.

Václav Havel was imprisoned from 1979 to 1983, but later in the 1980s Perestroika gave Czechoslovak dissidents a bit more breathing room. The world was put to rights in the pubs of Prague – and not just in words. In November 1989 the 'Velvet Revolution', with Havel and Dienstbier in leading roles, achieved a change in government. In December 1989 Havel became President of

Czechoslovakia, and Dienstbier served as foreign minister until 1992.

During his presidency, Havel did not abandon his old habits. In an interview with a Finnish journalist, he told a hilarious anecdote from his first visit to the United States as president of his country in February 1990. Havel wanted to nip into a local bar during his visit. He sat down at the bar for a beer and shooed his security detail away. Soon an American sat down beside him, and the two men started talking. The local man commented on Havel's foreign accent and asked where he was from. 'Czechoslovakia,' Havel replied. The man did not appear to know exactly where that was, but soon he asked a follow-up question: 'So, what kind of work do you do over there in Czechoslovakia?' Havel answered truthfully, saying he was the President of Czechoslovakia, at which point the American burst out laughing until flecks of foam formed in the corners of his mouth. 'That's a good one! Good one!' he exclaimed once he had recovered and slapped Havel on the back. 'That answer deserves a beer!' Havel did not decline, and as the men clinked their fresh glasses, the American announced to the entire bar that he was drinking a beer with the President of Czechoslovakia.

To the dismay of his aides, throughout his time as president Havel never gave up his habit of making unplanned stops in his favourite pubs for a beer. His bodyguards went along, but they could not make any special arrangements for the president's protection – nor did Havel want any. His guests also got to learn about the best aspects of his country. *Na Rybárně*, which had been Havel's local pub for decades, was located right next door to his old apartment at Gorazdova 17. As President, he brought the Rolling Stones there as well as US Secretary of State Madeleine Albright (who had been born Marie Jana Körbelová in Prague) to enjoy a Pilsner Urquell. Today, Urquell is still on tap at the same address. The menu has changed though, from simple fish dishes to Vietnamese cuisine. When Bill Clinton visited Prague in 1994, Havel brought him to the legendary *U Zlatého Tygra* (Husova 17) in the Old Town for an Urquell. The same beer, along with a few other Czech brands, was also on tap in Havel's third regular haunt, *U Dvou sluncŭ* (Nerudova 47), which is conveniently located just a few blocks from Prague Castle – the official residence of the Czech President.

Krakonoš Světlý Ležák

TRUTNOV, CZECH REPUBLIC

z Trutnova
od 1582

TYPE: pilsner
ABV: 5.1%
GRAVITY: 12°P
BITTERNESS: 36 EBU
COLOUR: 12 EBC

Trutnov is located in the northern part of the Czech Republic, near the Polish border. Václav Havel had close ties to the city, and he died at his country home in the village of Hrádeček after a long battle with cancer. Up to the Second World War, the area was predominantly German-speaking, and from 1938 to 1945 it was part of the German Reich in the Sudetenland.

The oldest documentation of brewing in Trutnov dates from 1260, when King Ottokar II of Bohemia endorsed the right of the city's burghers to brew beer. The local brewery, *Pivovar Krakonoš Trutnov*, was founded in 1582, and it is a medium-sized brewery in Czech terms. Its pilsner and light and dark lagers are sold mainly in nearby areas, primarily in the regions of Hradec Králové and Liberec.

Krakonoš Světlý Ležák is the Trutnov brewery's leading product, both in terms of quantity and reputation. It is an amber-coloured unpasteurized pilsner with a thick head. Its nose has malty, fruity and toffee notes. Its taste is malty, sharpened by hops. The finish is typical of Czech pilsners: dry and hoppy.

POLSKA PARTIA PRZYJACIÓŁ PIWA

AL. JEROZOLIMSKIE 42 m 100
00-024 WARSZAWA

PKO-BP IX O/Warszawa   tel./fax 275-422
Nr konta 1599-324988-132 tel./fax 275-423

leg. nr.: . . . .

miejsce
na
zdjęcie

imię . . . .

nazwisko . . . .

miasto . . . .

ulica . . . .   nr mieszkania . . . .

kod . . . .   telefon . . . .

A membership card printed in Pan *magazine generated a flood of responses, which transformed the Beer Lovers' Party from a private joke into a genuine political movement.*

XXI

Scouting for Parliament

Poland led the way in Eastern Europe's transformation from communism to multi-party democracy in the late 1980s and early 1990s. In the 1989 election the Solidarity labour union movement took all the available seats in the *Sejm*, the Polish Parliament, and Solidarity leader Lech Wałęsa became President. Poland was free – but uncertain what to do with that freedom. Once the initial euphoria had dissipated, citizens had to return to their dreary daily lives. The fall of communism did not bring West German standards of living to everyone. Quite the reverse. The conversion to a market economy was far from painless. Efficiency measures in the bloated state industries meant mass layoffs. The lifting of price controls on foodstuffs spurred inflation. The Solidarity movement splintered into several new parties, and politics started to resemble a noisy sandbox. The time leading up to Poland's first fully free parliamentary election in 1991 was characterised by disappointment and pessimism. As President, Wałęsa came in for his share of the criticism being lobbed about by the grumpy public at anything even vaguely political. Poles wanted change, but without knowing exactly what, and one sign of those turbulent times in the early 1990s turned out to be the

Polish Beer Lovers' Party – in Polish, *Polska Partia Przyjaciół Piwa*, or PPPP for short.

The Polish Beer Lovers' Party was not unique in European history. There were similar parties in the 1990s in Czechoslovakia, Russia, Ukraine and Belarus. The groups in those countries had policies broadly similar to that of the Polish group. Some seriously campaigned for economic reforms and temperance, while some were purely joke parties. However, the Polish beer lovers were the only ones who actually got into Parliament.

Opposition to the state had been a defining characteristic of the Polish national identity for generations. Ever since its partition in the late 18th century, Poland had had two centuries of governments that did not represent its people – with the exception of its brief period as a republic from 1918 to 1939. At some times it was occupied by Russia, the Austro-Hungarian empire and Prussia; at other times, Nazi Germany. The post-war Communist regime was imposed by the Soviet Union. Against this background it's no wonder that people's disappointment in freedom manifested itself in widespread political opposition. Some people took part in demonstrations against the transitional government. Some didn't care and let politics exist in its own parallel reality. Some made it into a joke.

Skauci Piwni, 'The Beer Scouts', was a comedy series shown on television in the late 1980s and early '90s in which a group of grown men dressed in Scout uniforms go on jolly adventures, fuelled by beer. The series was not a great success, but its makers earned their place in history with an idea they had during shooting: why not set up a political party for beer? They played around with the idea over a few beers. It still sounded good the next morning.

A lot of other parties were being set up in Poland in those days, too. The Solidarity movement had drawn together opponents of Polish Communism in the 1980s, but when their common enemy disappeared, so did the factor that had united them. The nation had a transitional government acting in the name of Solidarity, but in 1989–90 the movement broke up into a number of political groups pursuing different aims. The Social Democrats, Catholics, Agrarians and Liberals represented different wings of the political landscape, and they too had splintered into numerous new parties. They were already present in the first fully free election for the Sejm in the autumn of 1991. The confused nature of the political system was evident in the fact that 111 parties and candidate groups took part in the 1991 elections. Half of them were present in at least two districts, and a couple of dozen parties were active nationwide.

PPPP started out as an inside joke. The 'Beer Scouts' performers' idea was supported by the editors of *Pan* magazine, and editor-in-chief Adam Halber wanted to refine it even further. He drafted a semi-serious policy for the party which decreed that members would 'do their utmost to ensure that beer-drinking culture is good and leading the party is even better. Proper taverns are required in which people can have a beer in relaxed surroundings. The vulgar vodka culture along the Oder, the Vistula and the Bug can be countered by consuming beverages brewed with hops.' The reference to vodka culture was on target. Unlike its neighbours Czechoslovakia and Germany, in 1990 Poland was the westernmost outpost of the Eastern European vodka belt. The average Pole drank ten litres of vodka a year. Sixty per cent of all alcohol consumed was vodka, while less than a quarter was beer. Beer consumption (29 litres per capita annually) was around a fifth that of Czechoslovakia.

Beer definitely did have a long, colourful history in Poland. Its fertile plains were ideal for growing barley, and in the Middle Ages beer was brewed there just as in the rest of Central Europe. It also caused feelings to run high. In the city of Wrocław (known as Breslau in German), located in Silesia in the south-western part of present-day Poland, the fate of a few barrels of beer culminated in a dispute (1380–1382) between the Church and the city's secular rulers which is now remembered as the Beer War of 1380, though the enmities were fortunately of the non-violent sort.

In 14th-century Silesia, monasteries had special dispensation to brew and serve beer, but otherwise the city council had a monopoly on both brewing and serving it. The status of the local cathedral chapter was the subject of contention. The chapter, which was under the authority of the bishop of Breslau, was according to their own view comparable to a monastery, but the city's rulers refused to grant the bishop permission to brew and sell beer. When the city council, seeking to maintain its monopoly, confiscated several barrels of beer from the renowned brewery in Schweidnitz (now Świdnica) which the Duke of Liegnitz (Legnica) had sent to the cathedral chapter as a Christmas present, the clerics' cup finally ranneth over. The city's burghers were even threatened with excommunication unless the consignment of beer was returned. The chapter also banned church services in Breslau until the canons got their beer. The city did not give in. Insults and curses flew back and forth. The doors to the churches remained closed for over a year. A truce in this war of words was achieved only through the intervention of the Pope and the king in May 1382. The cathedral chapter and the city council promised to afford one another 'honour, worship, obedience and faith,' as the formal document put it. The issue of brewing rights remained unsettled for centuries.

Some six centuries later, talk of beer in Poland was more civilised – respecting the laws and regulations. In order to become a registered political party, the Beer Lovers had to collect 5,000 signatures of support. Adam Halber published an announcement in the autumn 1990 issue of *Pan* magazine about the beer party that was being established. A supporter's card was enclosed, which people were asked to send in to the office. The number of responses was astounding. Thousands of readers submitted the cards complete with their name, address and signature. They smashed through 5,000 mark and the Polish Beer Lovers' Party was duly entered into the register of political parties on 28 December 1990. The joke had just got real. The next question was what the party actually wanted to do.

The beer party started gearing up for the election. Janusz Rewiński, a comedian familiar from the 'Beer Scouts', was selected to be the party's chairman and figurehead. Deputy chairman Halber was in charge of practical matters. His draft platform was fleshed out. They wanted to foster beer culture by means such as increasing taxes on stronger alcoholic drinks than beer, simplifying the bureaucracy involved in opening a microbrewery or pub, and tightening up environmental legislation, because 'you can't brew proper beer without clean water'.

The party kept its fool's mask on in public. The bearded, paunchy Rewiński was easily recognisable and collected a lot of sympathy points as chairman, which brought the Beer Lovers plenty of publicity. Campaign ads showed him wearing his familiar scout's uniform, carrying a beer barrel. Rewiński wrote the lyrics for the party anthem, which highlighted the benefits of beer over vodka: 'Have a beer, and another, and a third / you can get a bit tipsy / No more of the hard stuff / so just grab yourself a beer!'

Behind the scenes, Halber quickly amassed hundreds of candidates. Some were attracted by the beer party's fun image or Rewiński's celebrity. Some saw the party as a fresh, liberal alternative. Even though the single-party Communist rule had only ended two years ago, many national parties were burdened by the breakdown of the Solidarity movement. The tough reforms implemented in the name of the transitional government put strains on the liberals as well as the social democrats. The beer guys had no history in the Solidarity movement or communism. They had come from outside politics.

The results of the October 1991 parliamentary election was as expected for the major parties. Bearing in mind that this was Poland's first fully free election, voter apathy was surprising. Just 43.2 per cent of voters went to the polls. Support was so low that even the biggest parties, the centrist Democratic Union and the Social Democrats, each garnered just 12 per cent of the votes cast. The other parties got under 10 per cent. A total of 29 parties made it into the 460-seat Sejm. One of the most surprising was the Beer Party, which received 367,106 votes. With sixteen representatives, they were the tenth-largest party in parliament. They were assigned seats in the middle ground of the chamber among the centrists and the right wing, in the two uppermost rows. A joke went round that their seats in the top rows, closest to the exit doors from the chamber, were because the beer drinkers needed the shortest possible path to the urinals.

The election results turned out to be a Pyrrhic victory for the Beer Lovers. Their remarkable success attracted interest from abroad as well, and the party leaders were bathed in the media spotlight. On the inside, though, tensions were simmering. The party's pioneers led by Adam Halber wanted to retain their original objectives and to look at the world through a beer glass. If economic reforms or environmental legislation enhanced the status of beer, they were good. But a lot of businessmen had joined the party following the party chairman Janusz Rewiński and they wanted to make the Beer Lovers a general party. The difference of opinion between the idealists and the pragmatists grew so wide, the party split in two before the new parliament even assembled. The ideological rift seemed almost logical in the history of this out-of-the-ordinary party. The press had a field day over this latest turn and quickly dubbed the two factions 'Big Beer' and 'Little Beer'.

The majority (Big Beer) was made up largely of businessmen

who had been attracted by party chairman Rewiński's candidacy. Many had joined the ranks of Beer Lovers specifically because of the party's lack of historical baggage. PPPP was viewed as an opportunity for change. Zbigniew Eysmont, one of the party's MPs who later became a minister, recalled: 'Few of us business-men even drank beer back then. Joining the party was just an easy opportunity. We didn't want to get into politics for politics' sake – otherwise we would have joined the Gdańsk liberals. Instead, we wanted an opportunity to create a new environment for business.' The thirteen-strong grouping known as Big Beer decided to officially call themselves the Polish Economic Programme (*Polski Program Gospodarczy*, or PPG). They quickly became a coalition partner of the governing centre-right and right-wing parties. In 1992 Eysmont served as minister without portfolio in charge of business development. While the PPG group no longer had any-thing to do with the original party or its successor 'Little Beer' by this stage the name of Eysmont's party was still PPPP, the Polish Beer Lovers' Party. Thus he has gone down in history as the world's only government minister from a beer party.

'Little Beer', which was left with just three MPs, did not ulti-mately diverge all that much in its parliamentary platform from the 'Big Beer' businessmen's wing. The original focus on beer became a reform-minded general policy, though in economic matters they were further to the left than 'Big Beer'. As a three-man faction, the beer idealists did not have a great deal of political clout. As Poland's political map was still constantly evolving, it can come as no surprise that the 'Little Beer' MPs split into two factions in the middle of the parliamentary session. Halber, the beer party's chief ideologue, grew frustrated by the way the party was being run and changed his allegiance to the Social Democrats.

The parliament lasted for less than two years. President Wałęsa dissolved the parliament in May 1993, and a new election was scheduled for September. The Beer Lovers' Party entered the campaign in fragments. The party's entire leadership had changed in the space of two years. The previous MPs were either standing on other parties' lists or had left politics completely. Two years of parliamentary responsibility seemed to have dampened the beer men's drive. Even though the party had managed to scrape together some national sports figures and coach for their candidate list, the last gulp left a bland taste in the mouth. They garnered just 14,382 votes, and with a 0.1 per cent share they couldn't even dream of getting into parliament. Besides, this was a different political era than just two years previously. The three main parties got a total of 82 per cent of the seats in the Sejm, and there was no longer space for protest parties like the Beer Lovers. The party went quiet, and at the next election in 1997 the Beer Lovers were finally removed from the party register.

Though the beer party's history was short, it can be regarded as having succeeded in its mission. Poland had become a beer country. In the space of twenty years, vodka's share of total alcohol consumption had halved to around 30 per cent. Meanwhile, beer culture had flourished, in quality as well as quantity. After Germany, Russia and the UK, Poland is now Europe's fourth-largest producer of beer. And Poles' beer consumption trebled in two decades to 95 litres per person annually.

Żywiec

ŻYWIEC, POLAND

TYPE: lager
ABV: 5.6%
GRAVITY: 12.3°P
BITTERNESS: 20 EBU
COLOUR: 12.1 EBC

Poland's brewing industry has gone the same way as its political parties over the past twenty years. The big ones have grown bigger, and the small ones have been pushed to the margins. The largest brewing company in Poland is SABMiller-owned Kompania Piwowarska (market share: 43 per cent), whose brands include Tyskie, Żubr and Lech. The Żywiec group, owned by Heineken, has a 33 per cent share of the market.

The city of Żywiec is located in the northern part of the Western Carpathians in southern Poland. In 1856 Archduke Albrecht of Austria-Teschen, a member of the Austro-Hungarian ruling dynasty, established a brewery in the city which would remain under Habsburg ownership until after the Second World War, when it was nationalised. Its location in the Carpathian foothills and related images of freshness are also in evidence on the Żywiec label, which features a dancing couple in national costume and three fir trees. The crown worn by Polish kings is a nod to the company's homeland.

The brewery's namesake beer is a corn-yellow, medium-bodied lager. It tastes of grain and malty sweetness, with moderate hoppiness. In honour of tradition, the water used to brew Żywiec comes from mountain springs.

Water was precious in war-torn Sarajevo. When the Serbs cut off the public supply, residents obtained water for drinking and other uses from the Sarajevska brewery's wells.

XXII

The saviour of Sarajevo

In April 1992 Serbian troops laid siege to Sarajevo, the capital of Bosnia-Herzegovina. Over 300,000 people were trapped in the beleaguered city. A month later the Serbs cut off the mains that supplied Sarajevo with drinking water from the surrounding mountains. 'Let them drink champagne,' as Marie Antoinette would have said. There was no bubbly in the besieged city, but the Sarajevska brewery managed to save the residents from dying of thirst.

According to the official interpretation of Islam, alcoholic drinks including beer are *harām*, or forbidden. The Ottoman Turks conquered Bosnia in the 15th century, but they were relatively open-minded in religious matters. During the rule of Topal Serif Osman Pasha as Grand Vizier from 1861 to 1869, the first commercial breweries were established in Bosnia. In 1868 Jozef Feldbauer, an Austrian, founded the Sarajevska brewery in the Kovačić district on the western edge of the capital. The Grand Vizier was even in attendance to taste the first glass of beer produced by Feldbauer. He liked it so much he thanked the brewmaster by returning his glass filled with gold ducats. Things did not carry on so well, though. Due to weak demand and economic difficulties the brewery halted operations on several occasions.

Cities in Europe's mountainous regions have not traditionally suffered from drinking water shortages. There is plenty of fresh water from the uninhabited mountainsides, and gravity takes care of the rest. Wells are not required in urban areas. As a built-up area expands closer to the slopes, water mains are installed to ensure the water remains pure. That is how it was done in Sarajevo as well. Water was piped to the Sarajevska brewery from the slopes of the Zlatište mountain south of the city. The problem for the brewery was that water from the mountain springs and streams had high mineral contents. Lager beers in particular needed softer water for their bottom-fermenting process.

At the Congress of Berlin held in 1878 in the aftermath of the Russo-Turkish War, Bosnia and Herzegovina was ceded to Austria-Hungary, even though it actually was still part of the Ottoman Empire. The new governing power generated enthusiasm for Bosnia's brewing industry, and even people from Sarajevo were despatched to Pilsen in Bohemia on the other side of the empire to gather knowledge. At the Bürgerliche Brauhaus (now called Pilsner Urquell / Plzeňský Prazdroj) the Bosnians learned about the properties of water from different sources and decided to follow the Bohemian practice of looking for softer water in the bowels of the earth. An auspicious place for a brewery was found right on the southern edge of the city beyond the Miljacka River, where the brewery discovered a rich groundwater aquifer a few dozen metres underground. The new brewery was opened at Franjevačka 15 in 1898. The beer's reputation spread as far as Vienna, and Sarajevo lager became a favoured beverage at the imperial court.

Over the 20th century the population of Sarajevo grew from around 50,000 to nearly half a million. When the last Yugoslavian census was conducted in 1991, half the city's residents considered themselves to be Bosniaks and 30 per cent were Serbs. Croats were around 6 per cent and a good 10 per cent of Sarajevans self-identified as 'Yugoslavians'. In Bosnia and Herzegovina as a whole, Bosniaks constituted the largest group (44 per cent), ahead of Serbs (31 per cent).

The fall of communism in Eastern Europe in 1989–1990 also

tore Yugoslavia apart. After Slovenia and Croatia, the tsunami of nationalism hit Bosnia, which had traditionally been a patchwork quilt of nationalities, religions and identities. Bosniaks and Croats supported the idea of an independent multicultural state, while the Bosnian Serb majority wanted the republic to remain part of a Serb-led rump Yugoslavia or Greater Serbia. Fighting between the government and Serb troops started in Bosnia in February 1992. While most people took sides along ethnic lines, the Bosnian army had Bosniaks, Croats and 'Yugoslavs' as well as a good few Serbs who were loyal to the Bosnian government.

In April the fighting spread to Sarajevo, and the Serbs quickly laid siege to the city. The government troops keeping the city under control had a significant numerical advantage, so the Serbs did not attempt a direct attack on the city. Instead they aimed to overthrow Sarajevo by putting the city under siege and bombing it from the mountains. They pounded Sarajevo with grenades fired from three directions. When the city showed no signs of surrendering, the Serbs tightened the screws by cutting off the electricity and water supplies.

Water pumping stations had brought water to Sarajevo from the surrounding mountains, mainly in the east. When the war erupted, all the water installations became the territory of the Serb troops. People could fetch water from the Miljacka River which flowed through the city, but anyone on the open riverbanks was a target for Serb snipers. And there was no guarantee of the water quality. Rumours circulated that the Serbs had dumped poison into the river upstream. People placed buckets and containers in the courtyards and on the rooftops to collect rainwater, but these were just a sticking plaster. Plus, summer was coming. There are very few rainy days in inland Bosnia in July and August.

The few private wells and springs within the city were nowhere near sufficient to meet the need for water, so for six months the Sarajevska brewery's deep wells became the city's lifeline. Fortunately, there was enough water. Over the decades, new wells had been drilled on the brewery site, the deepest stretching down more than 300 metres. In 1991 Sarajevska's annual production had been 748,000 hectolitres of beer. If that amount had been distributed to the besieged residents of Sarajevo, it would have amounted to over 200 litres of beer per head.

Public water taps were installed on the brewery premises and water was transported to other parts of the city in tanker trucks. Queues at the tanker taps were an ever-present sight in the initial years of the siege of Sarajevo. Residents also dug new wells, but because of the lack of fuel the work had to be done manually, which meant the wells were shallow and they did not significantly improve the water situation. At least the brewery did not suffer from a lack of water. It even carried on brewing beer uninterrupted throughout the entire three-year siege. The quantities produced were not huge, but the most important thing was the impact of brewing beer on morale. Sarajevans wanted to show themselves and the world that they were not capitulating in the face of force; life went on. Besides the water supplies, another crucial factor for coping were the UN airlifts that brought food and medicine to the besieged city.

In January 1994 a water filtration system was built in Sarajevo under the direction of Fred Cuny, an American aid worker. The facility purified the Miljacka River water to make it fit to drink. It took another six months before the water purification facility was operating at full capacity. The purified water was piped into the city's water mains, and for the first time in two years water flowed once again from taps throughout the city. Having done its job, the Sarajevska brewery's well water could be put back to its original use as a raw material for beer.

Although city was badly damaged in the shelling and 17,600 people lost their lives (most of whom were civilians), the defence of Sarajevo did not break. A ceasefire ended the fighting in October 1995, and the Bosnian government officially announced the end of the siege in February 1996, after three years and ten months.

Sarajevsko Pivo

SARAJEVO, BOSNIA-HERZEGOVINA

TYPE: lager
ABV: 4.9%
GRAVITY: 11.2°P
BITTERNESS: 20 EBU
COLOUR: 7.3 EBC

In June 1914 Gavrilo Princip, a young Serb nationalist, assassinated Archduke Franz Ferdinand just a few blocks from the Sarajevska brewery, in front of Moritz Schiller's delicatessen. That incident led to the First World War, which also ended one era in the Sarajevska's history. Before the war, the brewery had been one of the largest in the Austro-Hungarian empire. When Yugoslavia became its homeland, demand for beer fell, and it took until 1965 for the brewery to return to the quantities it had produced in the 1910s (150,000 hl per year).

The Bosnian War (1992–1995) caused an estimated $20 million worth of damage to the Sarajevska brewery. All of its production equipment was upgraded in 1996–2009. Now it produces 800,000 hectolitres of beer annually, plus a million hectolitres of soft drinks and mineral water.

Sarajevsko Pivo is a pale yellow, fresh, lightly hoppy lager. It is made from natural ingredients (water, barley malt, hops, yeast) with no preservatives. It was awarded the *Monde Selection* gold medal in Brussels in 2011.

Brian Cowen was known as an unpretentious politician who liked to have a Guinness or two with voters even during his prime ministership. Photo: James Flynn.

XXIII

The Celtic Tiger's hungover bellyflop

+26%, +19%, +28%. From 2004 to 2006 the Irish Stock Exchange index (ISEQ) recorded dizzying growth. Other key economic indicators were moving in the same direction. The Irish GDP doubled between 2000 and 2006. Unemployment remained below five per cent, even though workers kept flooding into the country, especially from the new EU member states in Eastern Europe. Things were going swimmingly for Ireland. They were also going swimmingly for Ireland's Minister for Finance, Brian Cowen.

Cowen had entered the lower house of the Dáil, the Irish parliament, in 1984 at just 24 years of age. The son of a pub-owning family from Tullamore in central Ireland proved to be an easily approachable, easy-going man of the people who enjoyed visiting pubs and had the gift of the gab. He became a key figure in the centre-right Fianna Fáil party and was first appointed as a minister in 1992 at the age of 32.

In the early 1990s Ireland was one of the poorer countries in Western Europe. Its per-capita GDP in 1992 was less than that of Spain, around 60 per cent that of Germany or 65 per cent of France. Ireland had been a member of the European

Economic Community (later the European Union) since 1973, but its role in the global economy had been mainly as a hinterland of the UK, a source of workers who left to earn money in Britain and America. And many ended up staying there. In a 2008 survey, 36 million US citizens said they were of primarily Irish heritage.

But Ireland's economic and employment situation underwent a transformation in the 1990s. Ireland implemented economic reforms at the start of the decade, and Brian Cowen was involved in his roles as minister for labour, energy and communications. Corporate tax on profits was cut to just 10 per cent. Financial regulations were dismantled. Corporate subsidies were increased, especially for technology and product development. With Ireland receiving additional EU support for things like education and infrastructure and having the youngest population of any EU country, conditions were ripe for rapid growth. Many large corporations relocated their European operations to Ireland. The economy was ticking along, and Ireland became an attractive destination for workers from abroad for the first time in centuries. Even its own nationals started returning home to the Emerald Isle.

From 1995 to 2000 the Irish GDP grew by nearly 10 per cent each year. In 1999 Ireland's per capita GDP even exceeded Britain's, with no end to the boom in sight. Ireland's economic miracle earned it the nickname 'the Celtic Tiger', placing it alongside the 'Asian Tigers' which rose to become major economic powers back in the 1960s: South Korea, Taiwan, Hong Kong and Singapore. And the Irish economy returned to growth much more buoyantly than the rest of Europe after the global recession at the turn of the millennium.

Brian Cowen served as Ireland's health and foreign minister between 1997 and 2004. In September 2004 he became Minister for Finance. Times were good. Computer giants like HP, Apple and Dell ran their European operations from Ireland. Intel, the computer processor manufacturer, and Google were investing hundreds of millions there. Tax revenues increased, the budget had a healthy surplus and the most challenging task for the minister for finance was to decide which major corporation's new site launch to attend on any given day. And while there might be clinking of cosmopolitan champagne glasses at the official openings, frothy darker-hued tipples would flow later on the nearby pub, as was the national tradition.

In December 2004 Cowen announced his first budget. Expenditures increased by nine per cent or €3.7 billion in the 2005 budget. Even though €3 billion of that was new national debt, everything seemed to be all right. Investments were still generating returns. Things still looked good. Ireland was experiencing the American Dream. Capitalism's success story had taken the entire nation from rags to riches. Only *The Economist* warned Ireland of the danger of a property bubble in June 2005 – the real estate price index had nearly trebled from 1997 to 2005 – and the government did nothing to slow that growth.

The finance ministry's strategic decisions were thrashed out in the restaurant of the *Dáil*, the lower house of the Irish parliament. Lunches there were described as boozy, and evenings carried on until last orders. But Cowen's inner circle continued slogging away at the nation's economy into the wee small hours, and when the numbers for the budget calculations started to swim in front of their eyes, they liked to lift the mood with a bit of singing. No taxpayers' money was spent on these Guinness-fuelled improvised economics seminars (at least not directly), as all the participants bought their own rounds.

The financial wing of the Fianna Fáil party were particularly keen to plan economic policy on Wednesday evenings, as the lower house traditionally did not sit in session on Thursdays. Understandably, contemplation, blue-sky thinking and excessive juggling of numbers can cause a little headache and even grogginess the next morning.

The heady rush of the economy was not reflected in the breweries' balance sheets. Beer consumption in Ireland decreased slightly throughout the early part of the first decade of the 21st century. The change was especially apparent in pubs. Sales of draught beer decreased by nearly a third from 2000 to 2007. While sales of bottled beer increased slightly, it was not enough to offset the trend. Increasingly affluent Ireland was taking its drinking cues from Continental Europe. Total sales of wine and cider were booming.

Finance Minister Cowen was not one to slavishly follow trends. He did not sip €20 cocktails in the trendy nightspots favoured by the country's successful young professionals, preferring to sup his Guinness with ordinary folk in the local pub. Though Cowen attracted good-natured ribbing for his unrefined nature, the general opinion in Ireland seemed to be supportive of him. This was also evident in his political support. In the spring 2007 parliamentary election Cowen was the overwhelming winner in his constituency. Fianna Fáil remained the largest party in the Dáil and continued to govern. People expressed approval of the budget Cowen had presented at the end of the preceding year which improved social benefits and doubled tax relief for first-time home buyers.

The following year brought changes in Brian Cowen's life and for the Irish economy. In April 2008 Bertie Ahern retired as Taoiseach. Cowen, as the party's deputy chairman, deputy prime minister and minister for finance, was a virtual shoo-in to replace him. In fact, by this stage Ireland's economy had already started to splutter and it was beginning to look as if his term as Taoiseach was not going to be smiles in the limelight. Cowen got down to work. He started to dissect the economic situation with his trusted inner circle in the same manner as before, fuelled by some appropriately nourishing drinks. (One nickname for Guinness is 'liquid bread'). The new minister for finance, Brian Lenihan, did not join their merry group.

In the summer of 2008 the government had to admit there were economic problems. When the credit crisis erupted in the US that September with the collapse of the Lehman Brothers investment bank, Ireland also realised that without swift, decisive countermeasures the nation's economy was headed for a crash. There were actually two men at the helm. In public, finance minister Lenihan had to bear most of the responsibility for steering Ireland out of the crisis, but behind the scenes Taoiseach Cowen was also doing his own calculations. The budget proposal presented in October was a respectable attempt to get the country's economy back in equilibrium, but many felt the pinch of its cuts. There were noisy public protests by unions, students and pensioners, but the wobbly division of work between the prime minister and the minister for finance did little to ease the passage of the budget.

In 2008 the Irish stock index fell by 66 per cent, unemployment doubled to 12 per cent and house prices fell by nearly 20 per cent. The banks got into difficulties. A long period of increasing tipsiness and a couple of years of intoxication were followed by a stonking hangover. Multinational corporations relocated to countries with more stable economies, workers once again went overseas to earn a crust and entire neighbourhoods stood empty. Support for Brian Cowen and his Fianna Fáil party nosedived. In January 2009 only one in ten people in Ireland thought the Cowen government was doing a good job.

Back in April 2008, when Cowen became Taoiseach, Ireland's leading newspaper the *Irish Independent* published a lengthy profile of him with the headline, 'Sometimes, nice guys do finish top of the pile'. Cowen was presented as an atypical politician who was not a social climber, self-aggrandiser or viper. In the article Cowen is described as outward-looking, direct and a skilful debater. He remembered his youth as a barman and said he had learned more in those years than at school or university. The pub atmosphere had stayed with him ever since then. 'You have more people drinking at home, then going out. But for me, if I have a drink, I have a drink in a pub. On my way home from a meeting, I would always go in for a couple.' At the end of the article the writer still hoped Cowen would be able to have a balanced life as prime minister, '. . . to entertain, as well as to lead. Over to you, Tanaiste!'

As the economic crisis deepened, the public's view of Cowan turned negative. What had previously been praised as his good-humoured nature was now regarded as silliness. Similarly, 'sociability' became 'laziness'. The press did not poke into his private life, however. Taoiseach Cowen's drinking only made it into the headlines in September 2010, when the worst of the crunch was over. Cowen appeared on a morning radio programme on RTÉ, the Irish public broadcaster, with a husky voice, and the content of what he said was not the sharpest either. Accusations that he was drunk or hung over were squelched, but the cork had been pulled. It was no longer taboo to say that Cowen liked a drink.

In 2010 Ireland achieved a dubious world record when its budget deficit was 32 per cent of GDP. For the sake of comparison, the crisis limit defined by the EU is three per cent and Greece, the country worst hit by the economic crisis, had a 15 per cent deficit at its worst. In Ireland in 2010, the reason was down to special bailout expenditures to rescue the banks. The stabilisation of the banking system as well as aid packages from the EU and the IMF created the foundations for a return to growth. The US news magazine *Newsweek* even ranked Cowen as one of the ten best-performing world leaders of the economic crisis.

Sporadic plaudits did not stop the slide, though. In early 2011 the unpopular Cowen announced he was resigning as party leader and prime minister. After his announcement, the *Irish Independent* summed up his term in office as 'the worst Taoiseach in the history of the State'. Their tune had been very different just three years earlier. How easily reputations can be lost!

Cowen took another blow in November when journalists Bruce Arnold and Jason O'Toole described Cowen and the Fianna Fáil party's beer-fuelled decision-making in their book *The End of the Party*. Details of their evening boozing sessions emerged, including the fact that Cowen and his cronies' bar bill before that fateful radio broadcast in September 2010 had been €3,600 ...

In the interest of accuracy it must be said that the blame for Ireland's economic crisis cannot be placed solely on Cowen's shoulders, much less on his drinking habits. The origins of the bubble lay in the economic decisions made from the 1990s onwards, and ultimately in the greed of thousands, even tens of thousands of people. The same desires for the good life and instant wealth fuelled the Dutch who got caught up in the tulipmania of 1637 as well as Wall Street traders in the 1920s, Finnish yuppies in the 1980s and Spanish property speculators in the early 21st century. People had taken the same risks before, whether they were drunk or not. Cowen consistently applied his party's free-market policy, and it did indeed accelerate the economy. With the benefit of hindsight it is easy to say somebody should have applied the brakes by 2004.

It should also be mentioned that Brian Cowen wouldn't even make it into the big league if we were to classify statesmen according to their alcohol consumption or the harm caused by it. In Russia, Boris Yeltsin's last years as president were overshadowed by his alcoholism but, on the other hand, Mustafa Kemal Atatürk's unhealthy lifestyle did not prevent him from transforming Turkey into a modern state. And don't forget Winston Churchill, whose whisky intake just seems to confirm subsequent generations' view of him as an all-powerful superman. It's easy for the victor to flash the 'V for victory' gesture, and it's easy to hurl insults at the loser.

If the Celtic Tiger's economic boom had ended in a managed downturn rather than a crash, the pints Brian Cowen knocked back would have remained nothing more than an amusing anecdote in history books.

Guinness Draught

DUBLIN, IRELAND

TYPE: stout
ABV: 4.2%
GRAVITY: 9.6°P
BITTERNESS: 22 EBU
COLOUR: 108 EBC

Arthur Guinness made a shrewd business deal when he leased the St. James' Gate brewery from the city of Dublin for 9,000 years. He started brewing dark top-fermented beer in 1778, and Guinness stout like the kind we know today appeared in 1820. The Guinness empire has withstood the Great Hunger years (1845–1852), the Dublin Easter Rising (1916) and the bloody war of Irish independence (1919–1921). One economic crisis was not going to cause the bottom to fall out of its business. While annual sales of Guinness in Ireland did decline from 200 million litres in 2001 to 120 million in 2011, global demand remained steady. The market grew especially fast in Africa, and in fact Ireland is now only the second-largest consumer of that black gold. Today more Guinness is drunk in Nigeria than in Ireland.

Guinness has become the role model for dry stout beers. Its taste is powerfully hoppy, robust and dry. The secret to its unique taste is toasted, unmalted barley. A nitrogen cartridge in Guinness taps and cans creates the bubbles which form its characteristic thick, foamy head.

The ultimate synergy between beer and football: In 2005 Liverpool FC, founded by brewery owner John Houlding, won the Champions' League, which was sponsored by Heineken – wearing match kit bearing the logo of the Danish Carlsberg brewery group.

XXIV

FC Heineken vs AB InBev United

In 1886 Henry Mitchell, a Birmingham man and the proprietor of Henry Mitchell's Old Crown Brewery, set up a football club for his workers. Mitchell St George's FC quickly became the top team with semi-professional players in the era of company-sponsored clubs. In 1889 they made it to the quarter-finals of the FA Cup, thanks to their enthusiastic chairman and his deep pockets, as one sports newspaper remarked.

Beer money continues to flow into football today. The sums involved have changed since Henry Mitchell's day, but so has their visibility. In the autumn of 2013 the European UEFA football league and the Heineken brewery group signed a three-year renewal of its sponsorship of the UEFA Champions League. UEFA is estimated to receive €50–55 million each year in the deal. In return, Heineken receives visibility in TV and online broadcasts to over 4 billion thirsty football fans.

Breweries and football have ended up in a symbiotic relationship since the very beginnings of the game. The English Football League was founded in 1888, and by the next decade several teams already had their own brewery sponsor. In return for their financial support, the breweries were given concessions to sell beer to spectators and advertise their products in stadiums.

And Mitchell St George's was far from the only team to be founded by a beer baron. One of the most successful beer teams in history is Liverpool FC, founded in 1892 by brewery owner John Houlding: 18-time league champions with five European Cup titles.

Throughout history, the same factors have explained breweries' particular interest in football. Marketing people might refer to them as 'synergistic benefits'. Football and beer-drinking are popular topics of conversation, and they share a key consumer demographic: men aged 18 to 35. Beer has a strong history as the drink of armchair athletes, first in the stands and since the mid-20th century on the sofa at home. When a club signed an agreement for the supply of beer to be sold at their ground, it was natural that they would cooperate with the brewery in other ways as well. The breweries' marketing departments associated football with images of bravery, passion and success. They wanted to those images to be associated with their beer as well, along with the supporters' allegiance to their team.

While breweries did seek to benefit in various ways from working with football, such as strengthening their brand, product loyalty and publicity, one can say it all boils down to one fundamental goal: selling as much beer as possible. The values of football club and league sponsorship agreements are generally secret, so it is impossible to give an exact figure on the brewery funding swirling around in football. In any case, the annual sum in Europe alone is in the hundreds of millions of euros.

The most outwardly visible sign of sponsorship are the adverts printed on football team's kit. For example, Liverpool had the logo of the Denmark-based Carlsberg brewery group on the front of its shirts for nearly twenty years, from 1992 to 2010. When the logo disappeared from the kit, that didn't mean the end of the relationship between them, though. Over the years, Carlsberg had become so deeply embedded in Liverpool fans' subconscious that continuing to sponsor the team's kit would not necessarily have brought the conglomerate any additional benefits. They might be able to achieve the same level of recognition for less money. Today Carlsberg lager is the 'official beer' of Liverpool FC. Partnerships have moved more into the realm of social media, where Carlsberg is presented as part of the 'Liverpool experience'. In the creation of customer loyalty, immersive experiences and creating a feeling of belonging are regarded as more important factors than merely maximising visibility.

In the 2010s, shirt logos have become less important in the major breweries' football partnerships as compared to the previous two decades. Across the five biggest European leagues, Everton is the only team to have an advert for beer on the front of its match shirt: since 2004 their shirt sponsor has been Chang, a Thai brewery. But other types of partnerships between breweries and football clubs have not ceased. For example, in Germany every team in the top three leagues has a partner brewery. Sponsorship has just changed its form. Now collaboration is more about the visibility of the partnership – and that extends beyond matches as well, such as in the breweries' own advertising.

Major brewing corporations are involved in sponsorship on a number of different levels. The prevailing trend is for the leading brand not to be linked to individual teams; rather, they achieve visibility as sponsor of tournaments and leagues, so all fans can engage with them regardless of which team they support. Heineken sponsors the Champions' League with its namesake lager; Carlsberg sponsors the English Premier League as well as the 2012 and 2016 European Football Championships. Meanwhile, the AB InBev Group supports the FA Cup and the World Cup.

The brewery conglomerates' other beer brands engage in sponsorship on the level of their own brand, such as by supporting national or league teams. For example, Jupiler is a beer produced by AB InBev which is virtually unknown outside the Benelux countries, but it is one of the most visible sponsors of football in Belgium and the Netherlands. The top Belgian league is officially called the Jupiler Pro League. Jupiler is also the key sponsor of the Belgian national side. League teams that partnered with Jupiler in the 2013–14 season included Ajax, Willem II and Sparta Rotterdam in the Netherlands and Anderlecht, Standard Liege and Club Brugge from Belgium. In other market territories AB InBev highlights other beer brands. For example, in Germany Hasseröder is a sponsor of Werder Bremen and Hannover 96.

Similarly, the Heineken group generally sponsors individual national sides and teams not with its namesake beer but with the group's other beer brands. Warka is the lead sponsor of the Polish national team. Amstel sponsors Manchester City. Even Napoli, from the heart of the Campania vineyards, has a beer sponsor: the Italian lager Birra Moretti.

In recent years the large brewing corporations have built up major entertainment operations around their football sponsorships. Fans can share in the experience not just at stadiums, but also at bars and on social media. Lucky supporters can win tickets to a match – or match tickets can be used afterwards to get into beer-related events, both in real life and online. The promotional campaign built by Heineken around the 2012 Champions' League and Carlsberg's long-term partnership with Liverpool both netted large numbers of followers, likes and clicks – and according to company intelligence, also had the desired effect on sales.

When people talk about smaller breweries' involvement in football sponsorship, the word 'togetherness' often crops up. When smaller breweries sponsor local sports clubs they are not after quantifiable financial benefits in the same way. The main thing is being part of the local community, being where the people are. Of course, they can target a large number of consumers via lower-division teams as well – for example, third-division matches in England and Germany attract an average of over 6,000 spectators.

There are also risks involved in sponsoring a sports team. Research has shown that negative images associated with a team can easily be transferred to a sponsor's brand of beer. Studies conducted in Sweden by Lars Bergkvist showed that supporters of a particular team shunned their rival team's sponsor. Fans of AIK, a Stockholm football team, were asked to rate various brands of beer. As had been hypothesised, the beer that AIK fans rated best of all was their own team's sponsor, Åbro. They gave the worst score to Falcon – the sponsor of their team's arch-rival, Hammarby. No similar difference among the beer brands was found in the control group's ratings. Breweries are aware of this alienation factor, and indeed they take it into account in their sponsorship activities. In Glasgow for example, football archenemies Celtic and Rangers have often had the same sponsor's logo on their shirts. Thus sponsors can ensure they won't be boycotted by half the city. From 2003 to 2010 both Glasgow teams advertised Carling on their chests. In 2010–2013 their joint sponsor was Tennent's, another beer brand. Again in the 2013–14 season both had the same shirt sponsor – C&C Group, an Irish cider maker – but the teams advertised different cider brands made by the company: Celtic had Magners, while Rangers had Blackthorn.

The ethics of sports sponsorship by breweries has aroused public debate in recent years, particularly in Germany. While the climate of opinion on alcohol-related topics has traditionally been more open in Germany than some other parts of Europe, the practice of combining images of alcohol and sport has sometimes been called into question. Breweries have reacted to the situation. In Germany, the Bitburger brewery, one of the main sponsors of the German Football Association, advertises only its alcohol-free beer in connection with the national team.

A New Zealand study conducted in 2008 showed that sponsorship of sports teams increases alcohol consumption in the same way as straight advertisements. The risks of alcohol misuse were found to be slightly higher among fans of teams sponsored by alcohol companies than in the control group. In a Dutch study published in 2012, alcohol advertising and sponsorship were found to increase underage youths' interest in the drinks, even though the marketing was directed only at adults. In their conclusions, the authors of both studies urged lawmakers to consider whether alcohol advertising and sponsorship of sports teams could be tightened up. The studies have not had any practical effects on things like breweries' sponsorship activities. In countries where alcoholic drinks are a natural part of the local food culture, sports sponsorship funding from breweries is perhaps not classified as one of the major threats to public health.

It is more ethically questionable if a sponsor is able to impose conditions on its support that conflict with a team's values or even with current legislation. Such cases are rare in Europe, but there has been an interesting test case in international football. FIFA, football's international governing body, has had a long partnership with the Anheuser-Busch InBev conglomerate. As the 2014 World Cup tournament in Brazil approached, the brakes were put on their collaboration by a Brazilian law that bans the sale and consumption of alcoholic beverages in football stadiums. Beer has not been available at international matches or league games in Brazil for decades. FIFA pressured the host country, and in 2012 Brazil finally conceded. By special permission, spectators at the 2013 Confederations Cup and the 2014 World Cup –tournaments were allowed to drink beer – well, Budweiser, at any rate ...

The upside is that breweries' sponsorship programmes often also include grassroots community activities. Breweries support youth football, maintenance of pitches and things like referee training. In their sports sponsorship, as in their other marketing activities, beer manufacturers emphasise the virtue of moderation.

Heineken

AMSTERDAM, THE NETHERLANDS

TYPE: lager
ABV: **5.0%**
GRAVITY: **11.4°P**
BITTERNESS: **18 EBU**
COLOUR: **7.3 EBC**

In 1864 Gerard Adriaan Heineken purchased the De Hooijberg brewery, and four years later he built a new production facility for the brewery in Amsterdam. The Franco-German War interrupted imports of Bavarian beers into the Netherlands in 1870–71. This created a market for the Bavarian-style lager Heineken had been developing. It was marketed as a 'gentleman's beer' to distinguish it from the ale favoured by the working class. There was a real demand for it. In 1873 the brewery was named Heineken after its founder, and that same year the production method of its namesake beer was firmly established. Heineken's lager won numerous international awards in its first decade. It is still made using the same original recipe, an important part of which is a longer period of cold fermentation than for ordinary lagers.

Heineken is a pale yellow, foamy lager. It has a fresh, fruity taste with medium hoppiness. Heineken is the world's third-largest brewery group. Besides its flagship beer, its brands include Amstel, Sol and Tiger. The Heineken Group has been the main sponsor of the football Champions' League since 1994.

THANKS TO:

Jako Arula
Daniela Brignone
André Bühler
Kenneth Cortsen
Emir O. Filipović
Larissa Fleischmann
Tim Hampson
Olli Heikkilä
Karel Janko
Michaela Knoer
Jussi T. Lappalainen
Ondřej Němec

Michelle Norman
Ulla Nymand
Lien Pleck
Annelies Rittgerodt
Paul Rouse
Olli Sarmaja
Georg Sladek
Manfred Straube
Sigrid Strætkvern
Elina Ussa
Adrian Tierney-Jones
Ines Zekert

INDEX

SELECTED BIBLIOGRAPHY

Alexander, J. T., *Catherine the Great: Life and Legend*, Oxford 1989.

Anderson, S., *The Man Who Tried to Save the World: The Dangerous Life & Mysterious Disappearance of Fred Cuny*, New York 1999.

Andreas, P., *Blue Helmets and Black Markets: The Business of Survival in the Siege of Sarajevo*, Ithaca 2008.

Arnold, B. – O'Toole, J., *The End of the Party: How Fianna Fail Finally Lost ItsGrip on Power*, Dublin 2011.

Badcock, J., 'The Fancy, or True Sportsman's Guide; Authentic Memoirs of Pugilists, vols. 1–13', *The Annals of Sporting and Fancy Gazette*, 1822–1828.

Barnes, D. R. – Rose, P. G., *Matters of Taste: Food and Drink in Seventeenth- Century Dutch Art and Life*, Guangdong 2002.

Bennett, J. M., *Ale, Beer, and Brewsters in England: Women's Work in a Changing World, 1300-1600*, New York 1996.

Brooks, R. J., *Kent Airfields in the Second World War*, Newbury 1998.

Brown, M. – Seaton, S., *Christmas Truce. The Western Front, December 1914*, London 1999.

Buhler, A., *Professional football sponsorship in the English Premier*

League and the German Bundesliga, University of Plymouth 2006.

Carpenter, H., *J. R. R. Tolkien*. New York 1977.

Cleaver, A. – Park, L. *Not a shot was fired. Letters from the Christmas Truce 1914*, e-book 2008.

Collins, T. – Vamplew, W., *Mud, Sweat and Beers: A Cultural History of Sport and Alcohol*, Oxford 2002.

Cross, A., *By the Banks of Neva*, Glasgow 1997.

Debre, P., *Louis Pasteur*, Baltimore 2000. (Translated by E. Forster.)

Evans, G. R., *The University of Oxford. A New History*, London 2010.

Glamann, K., *Jacobsen of Carlsberg. Brewer and Philanthropist*, Copenhagen 1991. (Translated by G. French.)

Glamann, K. – Glamann, K., *The Story of Emil Chr. Hansen*, Copenhagen 2009. (Translated by G. French.)

Glyer, D. P., *The Company They Keep*, Kent 2007.

Gordon, H. J., *Hitler and the Beer Hall Putsch*, Princeton 1972.

Havel, V., *Disturbing the Peace. A Conversation with Karel Hvižďala*, New York 1990. (Translated by P. Wilson.)

Havel, V., *To the Castle and Back*, New York 2008.

Hornsey, I. S., *A History of Beer and Brewing*, Padstow 2003.

Huntford, R., *Nansen. The Explorer as Hero*, London 1997.

Jenks, W. A., *Vienna and the young Hitler*, New York 1960.

Johansen, H., *With Nansen in the North. A Record of the Fram Expedition in 1893–96*, London 1899. (Translated by H. L. Brækstad.)

Kaiser, D., *Disident. Vaclav Havel 1936–1989*, Praha 2009.

Kershaw, I., *Hitler, 1889 – 1936: hubris*, London 1998.

Kershaw, I., *Hitler, 1936 – 1945: nemesis*, London 1999.

Knuttel, G., *Adriaen Brouwer. The Master and His Work*, The Hague 1962. (Translated by J. G. Talma-Schilthuis and R. Wheaton.)

McGann, B. – McGann, C., *The Story of the Tour de France. Volume 1: 1903–1964*, Indianapolis 2006.

Millard, F., *Democratic Elections in Poland, 1991-2007*, New York 2010.

Nelson, M., *The Barbarian's Beverage. A History of Beer in Ancient Europe*, London 2005.

Pasteur, L., *Etudes sur la biere*, Paris 1876.

Pokhlebin, W., *History of Vodka*, New York 1992. (Alkuteos *Istorija Vodki*, Moskva 1991. Translated by R. Clarke.)

Sharar, S., *Childhood in the Middle Ages*, London 1990.

Silver, L., *Pieter Bruegel*, New York 2011.

Smith, R. E. F. – Christian, D., *Bread and Salt. A social and economic history of food and drink in Russia*, Cambridge 1984.

Stechow, W., *Pieter Bruegel the Elder*, New York 1990.

Thompson, C. S., *The Tour de France: A Cultural History*, Berkeley 2006.

Tolkien, J. R. R., *The Lord of the Rings 1: The Fellowship of the Rings*, London 1954.

Unger, R. W., *Beer in the Middle Ages and the Renaissance*, Philadelphia 2004.

Unger, R. W., *A History of Brewing in Holland, 900–1900: Economy, Technology, and the State*, Leiden 2001.

Vaughan, H. M., *The Medici popes: Leo X and Clement VII*, London 1908.

Vlieghe, H., *David Teniers the Younger. A Biography*, Turnhout 2011. (Translated by B. Jackson.)

West, J., *Drinking with Calvin and Luther. A History of Alcohol in the Church*, Lincoln 2003.

Wood, I. N., *The Missionary Life: Saints and the Evangelisation of Europe, 400-1050*, Singapore 2001.

Wright, J., *Gustav Stresemann: Weimar's Greatest Statesman*, Oxford 2002.